ACCESS YOUR ONLINE RESOURCES

Every Child, Every Future is accompanied by a number of printable online materials designed to ensure this resource best supports your professional needs.

Go to https://resourcecentre.routledge.com/speechmark and click on the cover of this book.

Answer the question prompt using your copy of the book to gain access to the online content.

EVERY CHILD, EVERY FUTURE

Children cannot be what they cannot see so it's important that we, as educators and school communities, are children's eyes to the opportunities that are available to them. This practical book guides you in how you can reduce barriers in the classroom so all children can thrive and not just survive.

Chapters provide a springboard to view your curriculum through different lenses, identifying key issues facing disadvantaged children and assessing how pupils are catered for within school life. With a focus on belonging, relationships, curriculum design and community, the book explores evidence-based research and helps you to re-evaluate your curriculum to allow all children to succeed. Each topic is steered by key questions to encourage you to think reflectively about your own practice.

With case studies included to transfer guidance and ideas to your own setting, this book is valuable reading for primary and secondary educators, SENCOs and students keen to inspire and equip all children with the skills needed for the challenges and opportunities that lie ahead.

Louise Lawton is a Senior Lecturer in Education at Anglia Ruskin University, Essex. Louise has been a teacher since 2008, working in both primary and secondary settings, and now lectures and facilitates training to help colleagues and students to improve practice.

Rebecca Tarplett has been a teacher, Director of Learning, Acting Head of School and Nursery Manager in Essex, London and abroad for 20 years. Rebecca is currently an Early Years teacher and delivers training for Teaching Hubs as an independent consultant. She is also a Member of the Essex Early Education Branch.

In 2021, Rebecca and Louise founded the educational consultancy Tick Hub together.

EVERY CHILD, EVERY FUTURE

Visionary Leadership for Disadvantaged Learners

Louise Lawton and Rebecca Tarplett

Routledge
Taylor & Francis Group
LONDON AND NEW YORK

Designed cover image: © Getty Images

First published 2027
by Routledge
4 Park Square, Milton Park, Abingdon, Oxon OX14 4RN

and by Routledge
605 Third Avenue, New York, NY 10158

Routledge is an imprint of the Taylor & Francis Group, an informa business

British Library Cataloguing-in-Publication Data
A catalogue record for this book is available from the British Library

ISBN: 978-1-041-03484-1 (hbk)
ISBN: 978-1-041-03473-5 (pbk)
ISBN: 978-1-003-62400-4 (ebk)

DOI: 10.4324/9781003624004

Typeset in Interstate
by Apex CoVantage, LLC

Access the Support Material: https://resourcecentre.routledge.com/speechmark

We would like to dedicate this book to all past and present students.

CONTENTS

FIGURES

ACKNOWLEDGEMENTS

With thanks to the following people, schools and organisations who have contributed to our book:

- Joe Atkinson - Counsellor, teacher and psychotherapist (www.joeatkinson.co.uk)
- Yvonne Corkery - Head of French - Passmore Academy, Harlow
- Marie Saunders - Quadrant Outreach Lead, NE Essex SEND education team
- Ola Laniyan - Head Teacher, Temple Sutton Primary School, Southend
- Greg Waters - Head Teacher, The Bishops C of E and RC Primary School, Chelmsford
- Andy Scott-Evans - Head Teacher, Becket Keys Secondary School, Brentwood
- Liz Lee - EYFS Lead, The Bishops C of E and RC Primary School, Chelmsford
- Andrew Moffat MBE - Teacher and author of No Outsiders (www.no-outsiders.com)
- Kate Penfold - Head Teacher, St. Matthews Primary School, Redhill
- James Faulkner - Assistant Headteacher. Head of Personal Development, Careers and Computer Science, Great Baddow High School, Chelmsford
- Louise Boroughs - Deputy Head teacher, Burnham on Crouch Primary School, Burnham

Thank you to the reader who cares so much about helping our young people reach their full potential.

1

The Educational Landscape

Improving life chances for every child is essential – all children deserve an educational landscape that is broad, balanced and aspirational; one that opens their eyes to opportunities, to challenges and to experiences that help build them as an individual as well as a learner for a landscape outside of the classroom.

Pre-reading Reflection Questions

- Consider the term 'disadvantaged'. What images, experiences and assumptions come to your mind when you think of a 'disadvantaged' child?
- Reflect on who has played a significant role in supporting the opportunities in your life. How would the absence of this person(s) impact a child's ability to thrive?
- How might limited exposure to experiences and opportunities and basic needs affect a child's capacity to learn; reach their potential and also develop resilience?

What Does Disadvantage Mean to You?

Disadvantage is a huge challenge the education sector (and indeed all sectors) face. However, before we consider how we address this in schools, we need to delve deeper into what it means for each of us. When considering 'being visionary for the vulnerable', the following should be considered:

- We are all vulnerable at different times of our lives, but we might not all be disadvantaged. Contrary to this, we may be disadvantaged but we might not 'look' vulnerable.
- Those who have supported us the most have been those who have loved and guided us and been, in turn, role models. Take a moment to consider those who have been part of your network or village.
- A life with few opportunities and experiences to try things out could be described as lost 'self-actualisation'.

DOI: 10.4324/9781003624004-1

The Hierarchy of Human Needs

When examining vulnerability and disadvantage, it is helpful to draw on the work of American psychologist Abraham Maslow. Maslow's hierarchy of needs (1943) provides a framework for understanding the conditions required for individuals to thrive. He identified five levels of human need, beginning with the most fundamental at the base of the hierarchy. Crucially, his theory suggests that unless these foundational needs are met, individuals are unable to meaningfully engage with higher-level 'self-actualisation' or self-fulfilment tasks.

The five levels of needs are detailed below:

- Physiological needs: These are the most basic survival needs, including food, water, warmth and sleep.
- Safety and security needs: This level includes the need for security, stability and protection from harm, covering aspects like bodily security, employment and property.
- Love and belonging needs: Once safety is established, individuals seek to fulfil the need for social connections, such as friendship, family and intimacy.
- Self-esteem needs: This level involves the need for self-esteem, respect, status, recognition and a sense of accomplishment.
- Self-actualisation needs: The highest level, where individuals strive to become their best selves and live up to their full potential.

On both an educational and emotional level, we instinctively recognise what is good, right and beneficial for us. Even when priorities shift and we face change, this deep understanding remains – when visionary people are supported by generous provision in our school settings, true transformation becomes possible. We must first and foremost ensure that we are meeting these essential needs for our children and young people in schools.

Arguably, one of these essential skills is lifelong learning. Addressing disadvantage is central to fostering a genuine love of learning in young people. One in ten UK workers have changed their jobs in the last decade. Four million Britons have changed their job since the pandemic, and the most common age to make a career change is 31 (Department for Work and Pensions, 2026). Therefore, the chances that students leaving school will change jobs and careers multiple times is high. Given this, we need to equip young people with a range of transferable, lifelong learning skills and we need young people to be resilient.

Ensuring our most vulnerable are considered carefully is of paramount importance. Vulnerability and disadvantage are not the same: anyone can be vulnerable at times, and disadvantage is not always visible. Supportive relationships and positive role models play a crucial role in helping individuals thrive. Using Maslow's Hierarchy of Needs (Figure 1.1) as a framework for understanding these basic needs is helpful – if these needs such as safety, belonging and esteem are unmet, this can affect a child's ability to learn and reach their full potential. Ultimately, it highlights that while educational priorities may shift, our understanding of what children need to flourish remains constant, and therefore meaningful change is possible when visionary practice is supported by strong provision. We must keep this as the central premise and ask: What is it that these children, students, young people in this particular school or setting need first and foremost?

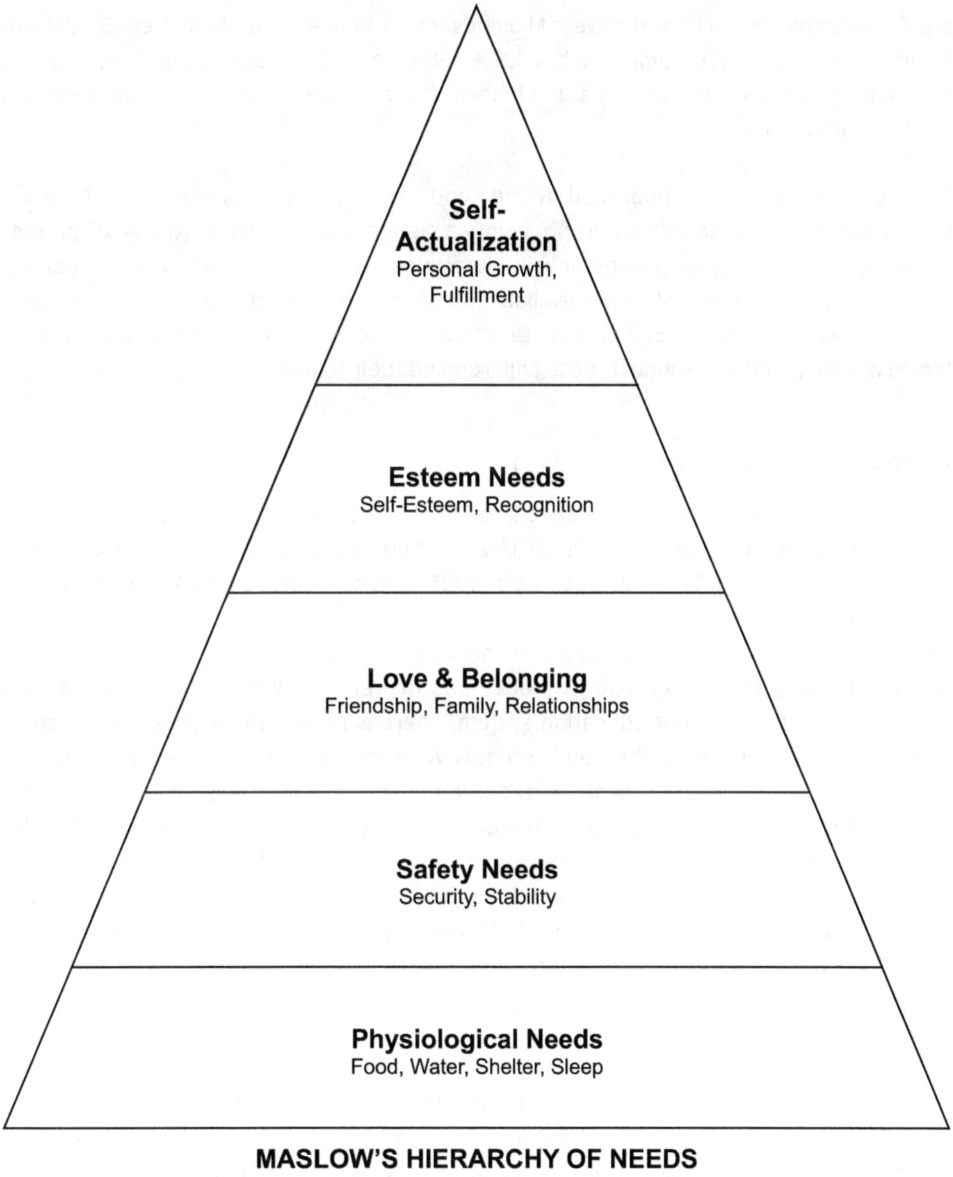

Figure 1.1 Maslow's Hierarchy of Needs

(Adapted from Maslow, 1943)

Changes and Challenges

In the last few years, educational disadvantage has grown (Education Policy Institute, 2025). This is the result of several factors during the early 2020s: Covid-19, followed rapidly by the war on Ukraine, impacted the number of families experiencing economic hardship. The cost-of-living crisis has seen food and living prices increase at a higher pace than pay. The Food Foundation dashboard (2025) highlights the poverty disparities across the country. For example, in parts of the West Midlands, more than a third of children (35.2%) are living in relative poverty, compared to 23.6% in the East of England. Meanwhile, 35.8% of people in the Northeast are living at the highest risk of food insecurity, compared with just 7.5% in the Southwest.

The 'Food Prices Tracker' published by the Food Foundation (2025) illustrates these statistics. The data, presented in a graph, paints a clear picture of deep regional disparities, revealing that where you live still heavily determines whether you can afford to eat well (Taylor, 2025). These statistics are available at: https://foodfoundation.org.uk/news/food-prices-tracker-october-2025. It is important that in schools we recognise children who are facing hardship and can support these children and their families.

Change in Demographics

The number of students in schools speaking English as an Additional Language (EAL) has increased over time. Over ten years, 2013–2023, the figure has grown from 16.2% of all students in 2013 to 20.5% of all students in 2025 (Lindorff, Strand and Au, 2025). The UK also had 110,000 people claim asylum in the year ending 2025 – this was a 13% increase on the previous year (GOV.UK, 2025). Of this figure (110,000), children account for 25% of those seeking asylum. Arguably, refugee and migrant children are some of the most vulnerable pupils within our education system. There is no central policy or guidance for how EAL needs should be addressed in schools. As a result, there could be significant variations in school policies for this group of students. This is concerning when we know that more than one in five pupils in England speak EAL. We know too that all children within the United Kingdom have the right to access education regardless of their immigration status (Lindorff, Strand and Au, 2025). Research by the Bell Foundation (2025) shines a light on the fact that many teachers do not have the knowledge to effectively support children who speak EAL. This, plus a lack of policy direction and declining resources, could well leave this group of pupils unsupported.

The Education Policy Institute has reported that disadvantaged pupils have, on average, lower attainment than other pupils, and this gap widens as they progress through their education. In 2023, 'the gap between disadvantaged and their peers at the end of primary school was 10.3 months' (Education Policy Institute, 2024; Idleman, 2023). They also discovered that children who are 'persistently disadvantaged' (children in receipt of free school meals for 80% or more of their school lives) have an attainment difference of 11.6 months by the time they reach the end of primary school. While this link between disadvantage and attainment is not new, the significant increase in disadvantaged pupils has arguably put significant added pressure on the education system. Speak to many teachers and they will talk about the effects of poor learning behaviours in their lessons. For example, pressures on teachers when children start school and are unable to use a toilet independently.

The general trend of statistics highlighting these needs continues. Since 2020, the number of families entitled to free school meals (FSM) has risen dramatically. In the academic year 2023–2024, pupils eligible for free school meals rose 23.8% (DfE, 2024) compared to the previous academic year. These statistics presented by the Food Foundation reveal this decline in food security. The data is available at: https://foodfoundation.org.uk/news/food-prices-tracker-october-2025.

The report, 'Households below average income: an analysis of the UK income distribution (March, 2024)' also highlights that the largest increases in household food bank usage were recorded for children.

Food affordability has become one of the defining features of poverty, and latest figures show just how differently families across the country are feeling that pressure. As food prices remain high, families are being forced to make difficult choices about what goes on their plates: fruit, vegetables and sources of protein are often the first to be cut back, leaving children missing out on the nutrients they need to grow and thrive.

Double Disadvantage

The Sutton Trust even go as far, in their research brief 'Double Disadvantaged' (2025), to coin the term 'Double Disadvantaged'. In the context of their report, the phrase is used to describe children who both come from a disadvantaged background *and* have SEND. These two factors, claim the Sutton Trust, intersect. These pupils face greater barriers. The term is applied specifically to the SEND system because socio-economic disadvantaged and SEND are interacting in ways that produce unequal access and outcomes. For example, we know from this report that 'those from more affluent homes are more likely to secure an EHCP (Education, Health, Care Plan). 65% of working-class parents spent no money on their EHCP application compared to only 29% of middle-class parents. 11% of middle-class parents spent over £5,000 on their application, compared to 1% of working-class parents' (O'Regan and Latham, 2025). Similarly, the report also shares that 'more affluent parents are more likely to use the tribunal system to secure an EHCP. 22% of middle-class parents successfully used the tribunal system after an initial EHCP rejection compared to 15% of working-class parents' (O'Regan and Latham, 2025).

What does this all suggest? More capacity is needed in mainstream schools to cater for SEND needs. How can capacity be increased so that schools can better support all pupils? Perhaps more early identification is key and thinking about the experiences that pupils with SEND have.

Given that the number of children with SEND is growing (numbers have doubled from 2.7% to 5.2% in 10 years) then this is surely a key area.

Is it an interesting correlation that the proportion of children now being homeschooled has increased by 15% in the last academic year? Data released from the DfE show in the academic year 2024/2025, the number of children in elective home education (EHE) rose from 111,700 to 126,000 (DfE, 2026). The data also shows that 16% of these children require SEND support with 7% on an EHCP (DfE, 2026).

From Social Instability to Classroom Reality

Rather than being viewed as an isolated trend, the 15% increase in elective home education can be seen as symptomatic of wider social and educational pressures. It is no wonder we hear terms such as a 'polarised world' to describe our current landscape. In a world where children and young people are growing up with readily available access to news about conflict and hardship, we see living conditions declining, causing life equalities for people. The effects of all of this are seen most prevalently on the education landscape - we see the effects of this on the issues teachers face in schools and in the classroom.

Class Sizes - Too Big?

The average class size in the UK is around 30 pupils, although this varies across different key stages. The Organisation for Economic Co-operation and Development (OECD), an intergovernmental organisation comprising 38 member countries, conducts comparative research into education policies and practices to address shared challenges. One area of its recent research focuses on the effectiveness of class sizes (OECD, 2025). In 21 of the OECD countries, the average class size is 21 (OECD, 2025). Arguably, smaller class sizes would mean a lower student to teacher ratio and would therefore create an enhanced learning environment for those students. This might also create more of a sense of belonging for the students, and potentially greater participation which could be beneficial for disadvantaged students.

It is important to note that while our education system cannot solve these conflicts and inequalities, it can help to shape the roles young people can play as global citizens in the future and provide space for young people to explore what sort of society they want to belong to.

A Wider View on Disadvantage in Our Society

Ironically, over the last decade, spending on disadvantaged groups, such as adult social care (18–64), child social care, housing and other – such as substance misuse and local welfare support - has fallen in Local Council Authorities (Tinson, Ayrton and Issy, 2018). But most of these services face rising demands. By contrast, the least deprived councils in England have increased spending on these disadvantaged groups (Tinson, Ayrton and Issy, 2018). The effect of this is that those who need the help most in real terms face declining services, and nowhere is this felt more than within the education sector when children arrive at school.

Fulfilling potential at school should not be affected by someone's background and how much their parents earn. Unfortunately, the reality is that this is clearly the case with the cycle of

The attainment gap between disadvantage children and their peers at the end of the Reception year of school is 4.6 months. This doubles by the end of primary school and it doubles again by the end of secondary school at 16.

5.7% of families have accessed a food bank in the last 12 months (July 2025).

The gap in attainment between disadvantaged pupils and their more affluent peers is 19.2 months by the end of secondary school.

Around 680,000 children in England live with allergies – and 1 in 5 fatal food allergy cases (anaphylaxis) occur in school – making children with allergies more disadvantaged than their peers.

Approximately one in four children in England and Wales are not toilet trained when they start reception class, with recent data from 2024 indicating a significant increase in this trend.

More than 1 in 3 children (36%) live in families that are living in poverty. This includes families with both parents working full time.

The number of pupils attracting funding in the 2025–2026 financial year was 2.2 million.

33% of children are reported as not school ready by teachers.

16-year-olds who are eligible for free school meals are around 29 percentage points less likely to earn good GCSEs than their more affluent peers.

Approximately two million children in the UK have speech and language challenges, which is about two children in every classroom. Poor communication skills impact's all areas of learning in schools.

Figure 1.2 Key statistics highlighting disadvantage and inequality affecting children in England (Adapted by TICK Hub, 2026)

deprivation being seen throughout the country. There are deep-rooted inequalities in our education system still, and yet the potential that education can have on a child's life is great. The fact that pupils from disadvantaged backgrounds are still half as likely to leave school with a 'good pass' in English and maths highlights this inequality, and although arguably there will always be inequalities, a child's education needs to do all it can to address this.

As a school, how are you levelling the playing field for *all* children? If one child is being supported by parents, educated to degree level and going to see plays in a theatre to support their learning at GCSE, they will no doubt have a deeper understanding and therefore achieve more highly than a fellow pupil who has not been to a theatre, nor seen a play acted out in real life and does not have a family that can support them in this way.

Equality and Equity in Education

Understanding the terms equality and equity is crucial in creating fair learning environments in our schools. What is the difference? Equality ensures all students have the same opportunities and access to resources, whereas equity recognises that each student's circumstances are different and that resources are given based on level of individual needs. This means providing additional support to address the need. For example, a language barrier or a reading intervention.

But what needs to be considered? Focusing purely on equality (the same resources) can cause opportunity gaps to widen. Equity involves providing educational resources to set up all students for success rather than giving all children the same resources and opportunities. Addressing every student's unique needs helps them all to reach their potential. That means schools must foster both equality and equity in their classrooms to make learning inclusive.

- Consider where and how you cater for *all* the needs of the students in school and classes.

Missed Opportunities?

Certainly inequality in education leads to reduced life chances and missed opportunities for children and young people to fulfil their potential. Schooling is so much more than grades and attainment (even though this is clearly important); we must address what it is our children and young people need in order to be successful, happy and fulfilled long after their education has finished. We need to look at trends rather than educating young people blindly, covering the same content and curriculum which was written over ten years ago. With ongoing barriers linked to deprivation, it's essential that schools are taking ownership for their communities' approach to tackling disadvantage and looking at what it is that the students need in that particular school, in that particular community.

Indeed, despite decades of policy attention, many education inequalities have persisted over time. There has been no change in the gap between children from more and less disadvantaged backgrounds in GCSE attainment over the past 20 years (Farquharson, McNally and Tahir, 2022). While GCSE attainment has been increasing over time, 16-year-olds who are eligible for free school meals are still around 29 percentage points less likely to earn good GCSEs than their less disadvantaged peers. But, in international surveys completed (which measure the literacy and numeracy skills of 15-year-olds), England is one of the best-performing countries in terms of school-age attainment. Yet, England is still very much in the middle in terms of inequalities (OECD, 2023).

Sadly, these trends continue and highlight the reality that disadvantage is posing on society. Indeed, schools are becoming so much more than just about children coming to school to learn. Reports from the National Foundation for Educational Research (NFER) go some way to illustrate this point. They report that a fifth of primary teachers spend their own money on meeting pupil's pastoral and welfare needs; that the 'share of pupils coming into school hungry, without adequate clothing, or equipment for lessons continues to increase' (Lucas and Julius, 2024). Likewise, the number of children starting school still wearing nappies is growing as well as children arriving at school wearing inadequate clothing (Lucas and Julius, 2024). In the same way, the Institute for Fiscal Studies recently reported that 'only half of pupils eligible for free school meals achieve a good level of development' (Institute for Fiscal Studies, 2024).

But what do schools and policymakers do with these statistics? Educators must consider the purpose of school and education more broadly but also what teachers need in order to get on and teach students. The most important questions to consider are how do we define disadvantage and who are these students in our schools? Educators will be unable to adapt the curricula in schools if they don't know *who* they are teaching. Let's unpick this further.

Defining Disadvantage

How do we define disadvantage in schools? The Department for Education (DfE) does not define disadvantage, but they do state on their website that 'the pupil premium grant is funding to improve educational outcomes for disadvantaged pupils in state-funded schools in England' (DfE, 2024). The pupil premium grant is financial support paid directly to schools for each pupil who:

- is recorded as eligible for free school meals or has been recorded as eligible in the past six years (referred to as Ever 6 FSM);
- was previously looked after by a local authority or other state care, including children adopted from state care or equivalent from outside England and Wales.

The grant also provides support for children and young people with parents in the regular armed forces, referred to as service pupil premium (SPP). This has been combined into pupil premium payments to make it easier for schools to manage their spending. Pupils that the SPP intends to support are not necessarily from financially disadvantaged backgrounds (DfE, 2024).

However, we know that disadvantage is much wider than this and these disadvantaged groups extend beyond these criteria. In 2018, a report carried out by the National Governance Association, 'Spotlight on disadvantage', revealed some interesting points. The report's key findings highlighted that schools should adopt a more holistic outlook when deciding how to spend the pupil premium, that there was clear variation in the quality of pupil premium strategies published on schools' websites and also that pupil premium usage is not the only determinant of disadvantaged pupil progress and attainment (Fellows, 2018).

From the schools and Multi-Academy Trusts (MATs) surveyed, the report revealed other criteria being used in schools to define the disadvantaged groups:

- Any child identified as needing additional support.
- Children with special educational needs and or disabilities.
- Those who speak English as an additional language or who are from an ethnic minority background.
- Pupils with a challenging home life.
- Those with prior attainment issues.
- Those with social, emotional and mental health needs.
- Pupils identified through a school's own socio-economic calculations.

A More Holistic Approach?

There might also be other groups which are relevant to your education setting. For example, the difference in attainment between boys and girls.

There has certainly been a plethora of reports published which look at the education system more widely. A national review into the existing National Curriculum was recently

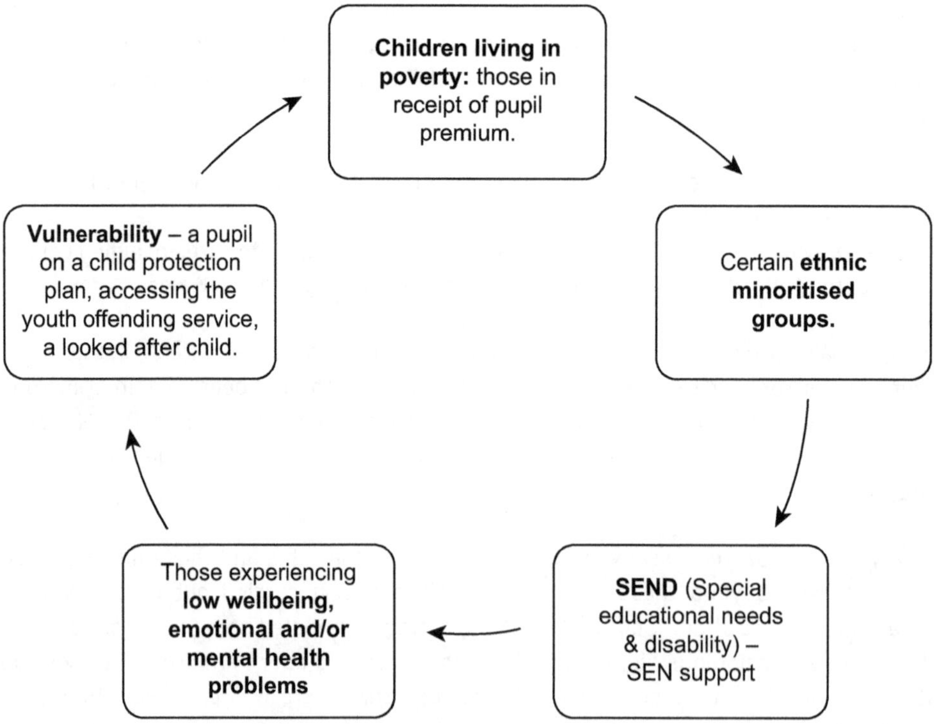

Figure 1.3 Widening the lens on disadvantage

(Adapted from National Governance Association, 2025)

undertaken, the aims of which were to assess the existing National Curriculum (published in 2014), to ensure that it is 'fit for purpose and meeting the needs of children and young people to support their future life and work' (Department for Education, 2024). Furthermore, the Children's Wellbeing and Schools Bill is currently going through parliament and is due to be published soon. This will go some way to protect children and improve education. The bill focuses on making sure no child falls through gaps between different services and that families can get help when they need it. One of the initiatives is to introduce free breakfast clubs to 750 schools as part of their 'Plan for Change' policy (Department for Education, 2025). The policy initiative aims to impact around 180,000 children, including those in the most deprived areas, before a potential national rollout. The schools that currently offer breakfast clubs report that they find the children who attend the club demonstrate improved behaviour, attendance and academic attainment (Department for Education, 2025).

Digital Inequality and Technological Change

Certainly, changes are constant, and as society adapts, people's lives shift in response. One of the biggest changes in education in the last five years has been technology. The shift to more hybrid learning, spearheaded during the Covid-19 pandemic, meant that the rate of technologic change was immense: 'The pandemic accelerated the pace of digitisation, automation and AI and exacerbated labour market inequalities, again underlining the need for action' (NFER, 2025).

But even then, during the pandemic the essential access young people needed to technology such as broadband was inconsistent and not equitable (Raihan, 2021). Yet we know the importance of technology. In fact, technological innovations are transforming our lives on what seems like a daily basis. We hear the terms Artificial Intelligence (AI) and see the effects of this already in our lives. Indeed, according to McKinsey, by 2030, 14% of the workforce worldwide (currently 373 million workers) will need to change their job because of AI making their roles redundant. Given this, our education system needs to plan accordingly if we know that these are some of the skills children will need in the future. An essential question to answer is how well we are preparing our students for this within our education system while continuing to ensure a focus on communication, language and social skills. This will not happen by chance; it will only happen by design and through a broad, clear and balanced curriculum.

Addressing the themes and issues of disadvantage is essential. We know that overall, disadvantaged pupils do not achieve as well as their peers, and those who are disadvantaged for the longest amount of time do worst of all (Education Policy Institute, 2024). Research such as this also shows these trends were evident before the Covid-19 pandemic – but we are at the highest levels of child poverty since 2011.

Education is not responsible for all this, but the role that people's knowledge, skills, attitudes and values can play should not be underestimated.

Chapter Takeaways

Reflections

- The levels of disadvantage have grown in recent years. Many reports highlight these inequalities.
- The difference between equality and equity and how we need to level the playing fields in schools are crucial.
- There are reports, reviews and government bills due to be published that have the potential to make significant changes to the education system, such as the Curriculum and Assessment Review and the Children's Wellbeing and Schools Bill.
- The need to identify those disadvantaged groups in schools is important, and assessing and analysing what it is those children need to be successful in in the future is essential for their future success. Before we can address disadvantage, we need to consider Maslow's 'Hierarchy of Needs' and ensure that we are starting at the very beginning with meeting basic human needs.
- Disadvantage has no set of rules, and it changes over time with circumstances.
- In schools we need to support disadvantage in staff and pupils to be effective.
- Disadvantage can impact children's long-term outcomes with impacts on wellbeing, attendance and future employment.
- Disadvantage is not just about money - it's more than this. It can include lost experiences, negative experiences, illnesses and self-belief.
- It takes a village to make change, and we can all be the catalyst for change in our communities.

Now Consider

- What is the difference between vulnerable and disadvantaged pupils in your school and how are they identified?
- What do the children in your school need, linked to Maslow's Hierarchy, to be successful in their life journey?
- What enrichment experiences do your children currently miss out on and how can they be addressed in your curriculum?

Enhanced Provision and Ideas to Support Learning

- Mentors and role models for disadvantaged and vulnerable pupils.
- You can only be what you can see - opportunities to inspire and visits that will open eyes and broaden young peoples' vision.
- School charters for non-negotiable enrichment.

- Experiences for all children to broaden horizons, develop key skills and inspire success.
- Parent workshops and cafes to support learning and engagement in education.

Further Reading

- Double disadvantaged reports of social mobility and SEND – The Sutton Trust
- Poverty in the UK Report – The Child Action Poverty Group
- Every child achieving and thriving (DFE – 2026)
- Future of jobs report – World Economic Forum

Bibliography

Department for Education. (2024). 'Curriculum and assessment review: Review aims terms of reference and working principles'. https://assets.publishing.service.gov.uk/media/66d196b7d107658faec7e3db/Curriculum_and_assessment_review_-_aims_terms_of_reference_and_working_principles.pdf.

Department for Education. (2025). 'Breakfast clubs' early adopter guidance for schools and trusts in England'. London: DfE. https://dera.ioe.ac.uk/id/eprint/41016/1/Breakfast%20clubs%20early%20adopter%20guidance%20for%20schools%20and%20trusts%20in%20England%20-%20GOV.pdf.

Department for Education. (2026). 'Elective home education'. https://explore-education-statistics.service.gov.uk/find-statistics/elective-home-education/2025-26-autumn-term.

Department for Work and Pensions. (2026). 'Get Britain working: Labour market insights April 2026'. London: Department for Work and Pensions. https://www.gov.uk/government/statistics/get-britain-working-labour-market-insights-april-2026/get-britain-working-labour-market-insights-april-2026.

Education Policy Institute. (2025). 'Annual Report. Education Policy Institute'. https://epi.org.uk/annual-report-2025-disadvantage/.

Farquharson, C., McNally, S. and Tahir, I. (2022). 'Education inequalities'. IFS Education Inequalities report. London: Institute for Fiscal Studies. https://ifs.org.uk/sites/default/files/2026-03/Education-inequalities.pdf.

Fellows, T. (2018). 'The attainment gap 2018 and the pupil premium'. London: Education Endowment Foundation. https://dera.ioe.ac.uk/id/eprint/30992/1/EEF_Attainment_Gap_Report_2018_-_print.pdf.

Idleman, T. (2023). 'Understanding the difference between equity and equality in the classroom', ETC Montessori. https://etcmontessorionline.com/blog/understanding-the-difference-between-equity-and-equality-in-the-classroom/.

Kindred Squared. (2025). 'School readiness survey: January 2025'. London: Kindred Squared. https://kindredsquared.org.uk/wp-content/uploads/2025/01/School-Readiness-Survey-January-2025-Kindred-Squared.pdf

Lindorff, A., Strand, S. and Au, I. (2025). 'English as an Additional Language (EAL) and educational achievement in England: An analysis of publicly available data'. The Bell Foundation. https://www.bell-foundation.org.uk/our-work/with-schools/research/eal-and-educational-achievement-in-england-an-analysis-of-publicly-available-data/.

Lucas, M. and Julius, J. (2024). 'The ongoing impact of the cost-of-living crisis on schools'. *National Foundation for Educational Research.* https://www.nfer.ac.uk/publications/the-ongoing-impact-of-the-cost-of-living-crisis-on-schools.

Maslow, A.H. (1943). 'A theory of human motivation'. *Psychological Review*, 50(4), 370–396.

National Foundation for Educational Research. (2024). 'The ongoing impact of the cost-of-living crisis on schools'. National Foundation for Educational Research.

NFER. (2025). 'The Skills Imperative 2035: Essential skills for tomorrow's workforce'. National Foundation for Educational Research.

National Governance Association. (2025). 'Widening the lens on disadvantage: Guidance for governing boards'. Birmingham: National Governance Association. https://www.nga.org.uk/news-views/directory/?Topics=Disadvantage:+widening+the+lens.

OECD. (2023). 'PISA 2022 results (Volume I): The state of learning and equity in education'. OECD Publishing.

O'Regan, C. and Latham, K. (2025). 'Double disadvantaged?' Sutton Trust. https://www.suttontrust.com/wp-content/uploads/2025/10/Sutton-Trust-Double-Disadvantage.pdf.

Raihan, N. (2021). 'Technological advancement in the era of COVID-19', *Open Medicine*, 16(1), 1–8. https://pmc.ncbi.nlm.nih.gov/articles/PMC7958161/.

Taylor, K. (2025). 'Food prices tracker October 2025'. *The Food Foundation*. https://foodfoundation.org.uk/news/food-prices-tracker-october-2025.

TICK Hub (2026). *Key statistics highlighting disadvantage and inequality affecting children in England*. Unpublished infographic/figure. London: TICKHub.

Tinson, Adam, Ayrton, Carla and Petrie, Issy (2018). 'A quiet crisis – Local government spending on disadvantage in England'. New Policy Institute. https://www.npi.org.uk/files/7715/3669/7306/A_quiet_crisis_final.pdf.

The Institute for Fiscal Studies. (2024). *The state of education: What awaits the next government?* The Institute for Fiscal Studies.

2
A Broader View of Disadvantage

There are several ways in which someone can be disadvantaged. Disadvantages are not always ongoing and can affect anybody at any time of their life. Disadvantages can be short term or last for a long period of someone's life. We should think of the different factors separately because it is possible to be growing up in an affluent family but still be disadvantaged.

Pre-reading Reflection Questions

- How do I currently define 'disadvantage' in the context of education and what factors do I automatically consider or overlook?
- What assumptions might I hold about children who are eligible for pupil premium, and how might these assumptions limit my understanding of wider forms of disadvantage?
- How aware am I of the long-term impact of early childhood experiences, and how might this awareness shape the way I approach teaching, support or school policies?

Defining Disadvantage

Disadvantage is one of the biggest barriers that we face in schools. In the 2025–2026 academic year, 2.2 million young people are recorded as being in receipt of some form of pupil premium funding (EEF, 2025). Whatever the reasoning behind someone being disadvantaged; whether that is poverty, poor early environment or ACEs (Adverse Childhood Experiences); evidence shows that being disadvantaged in the formative years significantly reduces children's chances later in life. Early childhood development plays a crucial role in shaping later life outcomes, including educational attainment at the end of secondary school, as well as economic and social outcomes in adulthood. A substantial body of evidence shows that policies aimed at improving children's skills during early childhood can generate long-lasting benefits (OECD, 2025). When effectively targeted at children from

DOI: 10.4324/9781003624004-2

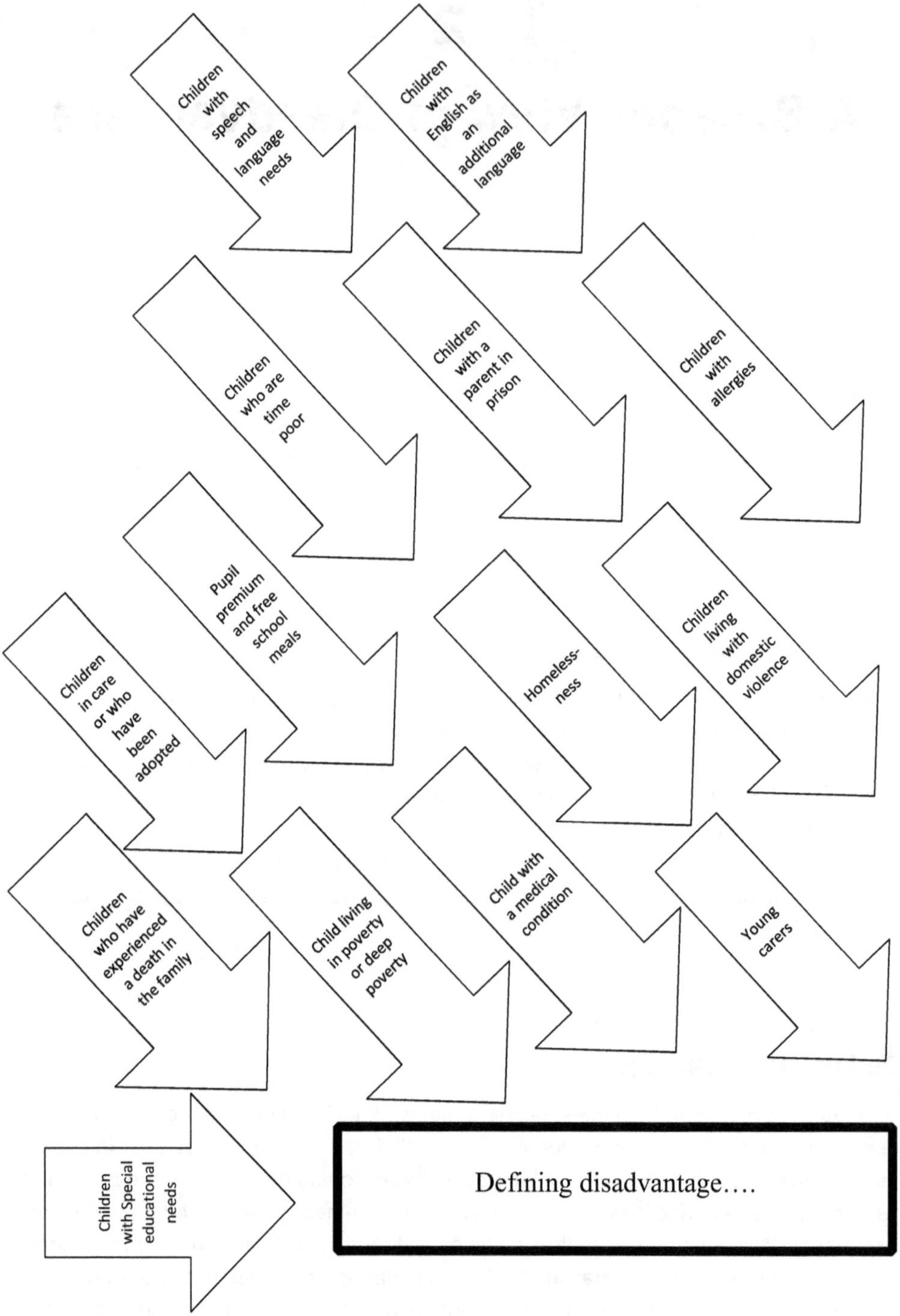

Figure 2.1 Defining disadvantage

(TICK Hub, 2025)

disadvantaged backgrounds or those at risk of developmental delays, such policies have the potential to reduce socio-economic and other inequalities in adulthood (OECD, 2025). Socio-economic inequalities in adult outcomes are influenced both by disparities in early childhood development and by children's early environments, beyond the direct impact these environments have on early development itself. In addition, developmental inequalities that emerge and widen between the ages of five and 16 also play a significant role in shaping inequalities later in life. If a child is not on track academically at the end of the foundation stage (age five) then their chances of being unemployed doubles at the age of 34 (Early Childhood Inequalities, 2022).

Pupil Premium

Although the classic interpretation of disadvantage identifies children who are in receipt of pupil premium, we know that to fully understand the depth of disadvantage we must cast our knowledge net far wider because this is, in fact, only the tip of the iceberg. In recent years, schools have become more aware of the far broader scope of disadvantage and how this affects children's life chances.

When considering pupil premium funding, it is important to recognise that it extends beyond pupils currently eligible for free school meals. The funding applies to children who have claimed free school meals at *any* point in the past six years (Ever6), children in the care of the local authority (through Pupil Premium Plus), those subject to special guardianship orders or who have been adopted, as well as a smaller service pupil premium allocation for children of serving and former military personnel. The primary purpose of this funding is to enable schools 'to improve educational outcomes for disadvantaged pupils in state-funded schools in England' (Department for Education, 2025d).

The attainment gap at the end of the reception year is 4.6 months, and that gap doubles by the end of primary and doubles again by end of secondary school. A key focus of your pupil premium strategy should be to intervene early to prevent gaps from growing. For the academic year 2025–2026 the Department of Education funding has been allocated as below and is expected to contribute to closing the national attainment gap between disadvantaged pupils and their peers:

- Pupil premium funding for primary aged pupils: £1515 per child per year;
- Pupil premium for secondary aged pupils: £1077 per child per year;
- Pupil premium plus for all pupils: £2630 per child per year;
- Service child pupil premium: £350 per child per year;
- Early years pupil premium: £302 per child per term.

With this in mind, it is equally important for educators to understand that the school does not have to spend the entire pupil premium funding on a specific child but rather use it to close gaps for disadvantage pupils. It can be used in the school where the need is more prevalent, if it can be proven to be closing the attainment gap between pupil premium children and their more advantaged peers nationally. This could be done in a range of ways from interventions and additional in-class support to opportunities for learning outside the classroom in the form of trips, residentials, music lessons, theatre or sports opportunities among other things.

At this point, consider how the pupil premium funding is used in your school. How does it directly benefit disadvantaged pupils, and how is this spending tracked, monitored and evaluated?

Widening the Lens on Disadvantage

Since 2020 and the impact that Covid-19 had (and continues to have) on education, schools have been more aware of the children who fall into the 'near miss' category: those families who are just outside the pupil premium funding category those children with working parents who can afford food and to pay the bills but have little left over for the incredibly important experiences, resources or opportunities outside the school doors that impact learning and provide the opportunities to consolidate learning and put theory into practice These children will be experiencing a level of disadvantage compared to their more affluent peers. Far more children fall into this category than those identified by the pupil premium criteria.

When we consider the reality of the broader term 'disadvantaged', it is becoming far more complex to define a set criterion because being disadvantaged can manifest itself in a plethora of different ways, and many young people are being exposed to multiple disadvantages on a day-to-day basis. When we widen this lens that disadvantages could include, we might also see:

- financial barriers;
- domestic violence or exposure to trauma;
- not having a family that provides care and love;
- not getting support at school;
- being born with a disability or having a disability in childhood;
- being a young carer or having a family member with a serious illness;
- low attendance;
- socio-economic background and home environment;
- ethnicity;
- health and wellbeing;
- immigration status, English as an additional language;
- personal circumstances including a parent in jail or a bereavement of a close family member.

When we are widening the lens it's also important that we consider ACEs. There are ten original ACEs, and it's important that we also consider these when we broaden the disadvantage lens.

These are identified as:

Abuse	Physical abuse	Verbal abuse		Sexual abuse	
Neglect	Emotional neglect		Physical neglect		
Growing up in a household where:	Adults within the home have drink or drug problems	Adults in the home have mental health concerns	Domestic violence is present	An adult in the family has spent time in prison	Parents have separated

Figure 2.2 Adverse childhood experiences

(Adapted from Asmussen et al., 2020)

However, in reality this is the tip of the iceberg with an ever-growing pool of adversities beyond this list.

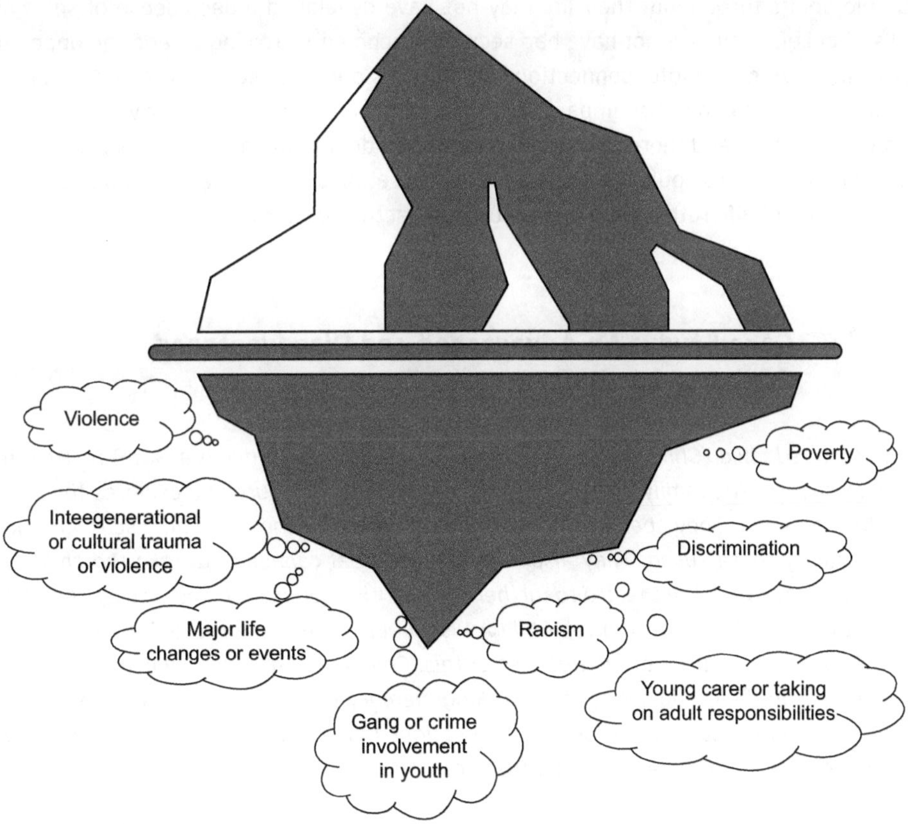

Figure 2.3 The tip of the ACEs iceberg – what lies beneath?

(TICK Hub, 2026)

A recent research paper published by the NGA (2025) looks at how schools can 'widen the lens' when looking at how they identify and support disadvantaged pupils. In this publication Marc Rowland explains that:

> *It is important to relentlessly focus on the impact of disadvantage on learning. Some issues pupils face may be beyond the school's power to change. But it is possible to address the impact these issues have on learning, as well as pupils' sense of belonging at school and in the classroom.*
>
> (National Governance Association, 2025; italics in the original)

Advantaged children have, generally, led a life to this point where their home and economic situation have meant that they are in a much more secure and stable position – mentally and emotionally – to be able to take advantage of opportunities as they arise. When they do experience a setback, they bounce back much more quickly, developing risk-taking skills and building resilience. With each successful learning experience, their 'advantage' comparatively grows.

In comparison, a child who has experienced hardship and disadvantage at some point or multiple points throughout their life may not have developed a deep sense of self-worth and self-belief. They may not have had secure attachments growing up and the opportunities to build up meaningful connections with others due to a lack of care and security. A transient lifestyle might also impact this, where they have moved regularly so not formed these connections and therefore do not feel as confident in themselves or as connected to their community; this could also include their education system. They could be seen as an observer in their life rather than an enthusiastic, active participant.

Case Study: An Advantaged and Disadvantaged Pupil and the Barriers this Creates

A teenaged child (Child A) from a middle-class family is studying a GCSE text from Shakespeare. The family places value on reading and literature and explores the text with their child. They spend time watching the movie of the play and discussing the vocabulary that is used. They also have the financial capability to take the child to see the play live in the theatre to further support their education and discuss the plot and the story. This in turn gives Child A visual aids to use when recalling key events and characters in their exam. Because of this, Child A has several visual and auditory strategies in their longer-term and working memory that they can access to support them in exam situations and secure connections that allow them time to discuss and deepen their knowledge though discussion.

In comparison, Child B comes from a split home where finances are tight. The parents are involved but do not actively support academic progress at home due to their own level of education and their busy work schedules. Due to financial barriers, Child B has not seen the movie or been to the theatre to see the play. Child B only has the chance to deepen her knowledge through what she sees and hears at school and has limited multi-sensory aids to support accessing working memory when it's exam time.

Through this experience, the advantaged child is further advantaged, and the disadvantaged child is further disadvantaged - creating a cycle of disadvantage.

Case study question: What practical changes could schools make to interrupt this cycle of advantage and disadvantage when teaching core texts such as Shakespeare?

Food and Friendship

Recent government policies have committed to supporting food poverty and childcare provision, with the current government committing to offer a free breakfast club for all primary aged pupils by September 2026. In April 2024 the government announced that they would be rolling out their landmark breakfast club programme to 750 schools as part of their 'Plan for Change' policy (2024). The project hopes to impact around 180,000 children, including 67,000 in the most deprived areas before the national rollout, which will see inclusivity in breakfast provision for all families, with the aim to raise barriers and offer opportunities, as well as tackle the impact of child poverty. Currently, schools that offer breakfast clubs report that they find that children who attend the club demonstrate improved behaviour, attendance and academic attainment (Department for Education, 2025b).

Other strategies that have been put forward to support both disadvantaged pupils and their families along with wider school communities include:

- Opening more than 3,000 additional nursery places and using available space in primary schools to enable this expansion.
- Limiting the number of branded school uniform items (Department for Education, 2025a).

Absence and Separation

Children of all ages can experience absence and separation for a wide range of reasons. Family separation may occur either by choice or through circumstances beyond an individual's control.

Voluntary separation may be chosen to allow individuals or families time apart for personal growth, reflection or to reassess relationships, particularly when partners are

Figure 2.4 Extract from the government 'Plan for Change'

(Prime Minister's Office, 2024)

experiencing issues such as frequent conflict, lack of commitment, infidelity or financial difficulties. Temporary separation can provide space and respite to reduce stress, clarify emotions, explore reconciliation or prepare for divorce by addressing practical matters such as finances, housing and childcare arrangements. Families may also live apart due to work or educational demands, including military service, employment abroad or children attending university or boarding school, while some adult children may distance themselves from parents to address unresolved trauma, abuse or neglect and just pursue healthier lives.

In contrast, involuntary separation typically results from external forces or crises, such as domestic violence, mental health or substance abuse issues, incarceration, immigration policies, child welfare interventions, serious illness or prolonged hospitalisation or death, all of which can profoundly affect family relationships and dynamics. Whether children are experiencing voluntary or involuntary separations, these periods of time can lead to struggle with emotional attachments and a sense of abandonment, anger, worry and anxiety. During this period of time, they may need secure adults who can offer additional support to navigate the situation.

Why is it important to bear this in mind? Children's experiences of absence and separation can significantly influence their capacity to learn. Pupils who are coping with separation may experience anxiety and a range of other attachment issues which could cause challenges with concentration. Without an awareness of these underlying factors, such behaviours may be misunderstood or misinterpreted as disengagement or poor behaviour.

Jail and Separation

A few years ago, we worked with a school in a South Essex town who were supporting a child whose father was in jail. At this time, we realised that there was very little support available for practitioners, children or families in this position. With the help of Joe Atkinson (a certified psychotherapist andteacher) we were able to unlock a deeper understanding of the barriers the child was facing to ensure that the family were well supported.

Case Study: Separation, Fight, Flight and Feelings

Joe Atkinson – Joe Atkinson Counselling and psychotherapy

Johnny is a 6-year-old boy who is dealing with an incarcerated parent.

Separation evokes primal emotions in us, and before the ages of at least 5-7 they will feel these emotions one at a time. The primary emotions are frustration, alarm and a seeking response. Johnny's mum had told him that she was on a long holiday, and he had no idea she was in prison for what turned out to be three months. This also meant that he would not be able to visit his mum while in jail. Johnny would stay with his grandparents while mum was away and have minimal contact with mum, and his grandparents would tell Johnny that his mum was away on a long holiday. My approach is an attachment-based developmental one which means that our focus was on inviting these core primary emotions to come out in play where they could be safe, not get him into any trouble, normalised and seen compassionately. Johnny was drawn to games of hide and seek, hiding figures in the sand and finding them again. He would occasionally mess the room up completely and put everything out of place, throwing things around the room. His grandparents found it hard to welcome these separation emotions safely, and having a space to do so allowed Johnny to process these emotions safely, making sense of his experience.

Case study question: How might a child's play behaviour be understood as expressions of separation, fight or flight responses, and what is the adult's role in responding with safety and compassion?

When we consider a child with a parent in jail, we must understand that they are disadvantaged even if, on the surface, their home life looks settled and financially they are well supported. Let's start by looking at some statistics behind the children involved in these involuntary separations.

Did you know that it is estimated that, in England and Wales, 200,000 children have a parent sent to jail each year (GOV.UK, 2026)? However, the National Information Centre on Children of Offenders (NICCO) estimates that this figure is closer to 310,000, and it has been reported that around 10,000 children visit a parent or relative in a public prison every week.

We must be aware of this situation so we can be prepared to offer our guidance and unbiased support and advice. At the end of this chapter, we have referenced some books that support working with children in this situation. Beyond this surface-level data, the statistics get even more gloomy. Murray and Farrington (2009) report that 65% of boys with a parent convicted and sentenced to jail will, in later life, go on to be an offender themselves. Alongside this, research shows that 25% of children with a parent in prison are at risk of increased mental health problems including depression, anxiety, eating and sleeping disorders. Parental imprisonment is also associated with children suffering from Adverse Childhood Experiences, which we have already touched upon, as well as negative school experiences including poor attendance and truanting, bullying and failure to achieve and thrive in the education system. We also know that children with a parent in prison are disproportionately represented among young offenders and the population of children who are in care (Nicco, 2026).

Barnardo's children's charity is one of the few charities in the UK that work specifically with children who have a parent in jail. Through research they have found that for children and young people who have a parent or relative in jail, the impacts can lead to (but are not limited to):

- poor physical and mental health;
- breakdown/lack of support networks (especially if the relative now in prison acted as a primary carer);
- significant trauma if they witnessed elements of criminal activity, and even the arrest of their relative;
- feelings of loss or rejection;
- fear of being stigmatised and judged by the 'prisoner' label;
- additional care responsibilities placed on the child;
- an effect on school (an absence from education and/or lower school grades).

(Barnardo's, 2026)

When working with or supporting a child who has a parent or close relative in prison, it is essential to work collaboratively with the remaining parent or carers to ensure consistent and clear communication. Children in these circumstances should be told the truth, even at a very young age, as honesty is vital for maintaining trust between the child and those within their support network. While these conversations can be challenging, it is important to communicate in an age-appropriate way and to keep channels of dialogue open. Children should also be given opportunities to express their feelings and be reassured that their emotions are valid. When having these discussions, the following tips may be helpful:

- Ensure conversations take place in a safe space where the child will feel secure in opening up about their feelings and emotions, whether this is a safe undisturbed place in school or outside the school setting;
- Ensure that the child understands that their feelings are valid, whatever they are. Older children may feel more anger and resentment than younger children;
- Ensure the child knows that this situation is not their fault;
- Focus on what support they can access and how they are feeling, rather than the offence of the person who is in custody;
- Ensure the child knows there is someone they can talk to and they have access to the support they need. It's important to ensure that the child in question knows how to access this support when they need it;
- Check in regularly with the child and family to support them. Children should have time to reflect on the events and process them. They should be given the choice of whether to visit the relative or not. This should be discussed with the other parent/carer, and a plan should be developed to support the children before, during and after a visitation.

Let's now explore other factors that link to separation and can put children in a position of disadvantage.

Separation and the resulting trauma are not experienced only by children with a parent in prison. Children can be separated from their families for a variety of reasons, including - but not limited to - divorce, the death of a family member or a parent's work commitments. At the heart of the disadvantage in all these situations lies the experience of separation, presented in different forms.

Separation and Divorce

Now consider children from a family that are experiencing parental separation or divorce. The children are often unsettled and unsure of their place in their family. They may be moving between homes, travelling to school differently and they may no longer be able to attend groups or clubs that are familiar to them due to financial restrictions, time, split homes or parental commitments. Research shows that children who have divorced or separated parents have, on average, more issues surrounding behaviour, lower levels of wellbeing and poorer educational outcomes than those children who have families that remain as a unit, with boys being more significantly affected than girls (Kalmijn, 2023).

For children from separated families, the impact of separation extends beyond emotional challenges to include economic pressures that create an additional layer of disadvantage. Many of these children do not qualify for pupil premium funding, yet they may still be living at or near the poverty line, as single parents face the financial strain of covering bills, rent or mortgages and utilities for two households. Research from the University of Sheffield concluded that single parent families are twice as likely to use food banks than married parent families, with single parent households twice as likely to experience food insecurity in Britain (Trussell, 2026).

In 2023-2024, 65% of support from Trussell Trust Foodbanks went to families with children, and in January 2024, 35% of single-adult households with children experienced food insecurity. In 2025, children continued to receive a disproportionate share of foodbank support: 10% of food parcels were provided to families with children aged 0-4, despite this age group representing only 5% of the UK population, while 16% of parcels went to families with children aged 5-11, who make up just 8% of the population. In contrast, only 3% of food parcels were distributed to people over 65, even though they constitute 18% of the population (Trussell Trust, 2026).

Schools need to be aware of, and monitor, which families could be on this breadline margin – those that do not quite meet the criteria for pupil premium funding but, once bills are paid, are very much at a financial disadvantage.

Take a moment to consider these questions in relation to your school or class:

- Are schools aware of those children who do not ever attend clubs – why is this?
- What about those children who do not attend school events?
- How are schools tracking and supporting these 'cusp' families to ensure that all children are having the best possible start?

For many children, schools represent their only second chance and for some, their first and only opportunity.

Death and Bereavement

Involuntary separation caused by death and bereavement can have significant emotional and psychological effects, and children often require additional support to navigate the changes and transitions in their life. Dealing with the death of a close family member or friend can be one of the most traumatic experiences a child can experience, and this will, of course, lead to trauma and separation which can impact them. On average one in 29 children experience the death of a parent or carer before leaving primary school. Put simply, on average, this is one child in every class in an average primary school in England, yet many schools do not have bereavement policies or staff with specific training in place (Winston's Wish, 2026). Chapter 8 includes a link to a template bereavement policy.

It is important that when supporting a child or family who have experienced a bereavement that staff are well trained to deal with this, that they understand what grief is and the common responses that children and young people may have when making sense of death. Did you know that the charity Winston's Wish offer free training on bereavement for schools? Free training can be found here: https://winstonswish.org/bereavement-training-courses-schools/

Other Considerations

Does your school have an up-to-date bereavement policy? If not, perhaps this is something to consider. A bereavement policy is a policy that no school wishes to ever have to use. However, in the event of a bereavement happening, whether it is sudden or something that has been expected, having a policy in place will enable a school to effectively support children and families, immediately reflecting the school's ethos, values and culture. During a period of bereavement, emotions are heightened for all involved and a bereavement policy takes away some of the emotion – it is clear, concise and allows steps and processes to happen quickly and effectively while considering the needs and wishes of the family in question. A school's policy should help staff feel confident working with, supporting and nurturing bereaved colleagues.

A school bereavement policy should include:

- Grief – a wider definition of what this is and how it could present in adults and children (and the stages of grief too).
- Communication – how the death is communicated to the school staff, families and wider community.
- Critical incidents – how they are managed and who will be responsible for the different roles that this involves.
- Liaising with families – how this is done and who is involved.
- Training – the training for staff and how this impacts the support given.
- Details – those who are available to support children and families (for example school counsellors).
- Support – details on how the school intends to support students, staff and families including time off, returning to school or work and liaising with the wider community.
- Wider support – details of local and national support groups, for example Winston's Wish.

Please refer to Chapter 8, for a template bereavement policy.

Work and Cultural Separation

Other hidden disadvantages include families separated by work or culture. Are you aware of families within your community who are separated by work or culture? This could be parents working abroad regularly during the week, long business trips or families where a parent travels for long periods of time including as part of the military. Forces (military) families are in receipt of the lower level of service pupil premium but should be monitored closely as their needs will differ greatly from those in the classic pupil premium group. Research indicates that while many forces families develop resilience, the frequent, often unpredictable and sometimes long-term separations of family life often result in significant challenges in emotional wellbeing, family dynamics and daily life management, The Forces Children's Education (FCE) team have created a tool kit to support schools working with the children of Armed Forces personnel. National Transitions Officer Carolyn MacLeod, who runs the FCE website and who works on behalf of the Association of Directors of Education (ADES) to support and advise Armed Forces families, advises that:

> The Toolkit was developed in collaboration with teachers who have a wealth of experience and knowledge, and in response to specific questions for more information. I think all staff will appreciate this resource.
>
> (Forces Children's Education, 2026)

If you are working in a forces school or a school which has a high percentage of military children it is important that you consider the impact of deployment on these children – do they have role models to talk to and are they taking on added responsibility to support their family when a parent is on a deployment?

The 'Apart: Not Alone' local impact grant programme was set up by the Armed Forces Covenant Trust Fund with the aim to mitigate the impact of service-related separation for families of serving personnel and reservists and is open for applications from charities and local authorities. For more information see: www.covenantfund.co.uk

Time Poverty, Separation and Disadvantage

Time poverty is less explored than classic disadvantage but can impact children from all backgrounds in similar ways. Families do not always have the time to meet the needs and responsibility of their family. There are multiple factors that can lead to a child suffering from time poverty, including parents having to balance multiple jobs or caring responsibilities. Other reasons might include parents having long commutes to work, thus meaning children spend most of the day in child care, along with inflexible working schedules. There are also factors including parents (or children) being care givers to family members. Action for Children (2025) report that around 1 in 5 children are young carers; that is around 800,000 young carers aged 11–16 in England alone and over 1 million young carers across the UK. In the UK, a young carer is defined as a person under the age of 18 who regularly provides care for a family member or friend with an illness, disability, mental health condition or substance misuse problem, taking on practical, physical or emotional responsibilities (Carers Trust, 2026). Individuals aged 16–25 who carry out similar caring roles are referred to as young adult carers. According to organisations such as Barnardo's, Carers Trust, and Action for Children, young carers often support parents, siblings or other relatives and may carry out a range of tasks. These might include cooking, cleaning, personal care and providing emotional support, frequently without recognising themselves as carers.

Young carers often take on a broad range of responsibilities, including practical, physical and emotional tasks. These may involve household duties such as cooking, cleaning and shopping; providing physical assistance, for example helping someone to get out of bed; and offering emotional support by listening to or comforting a distressed family member. Young carers may also be responsible for personal care, managing household finances, collecting prescriptions, supporting medication routines, assisting with communication and caring for younger siblings. Schools have a vital role in identifying and supporting young carers and, where appropriate, working with external agencies to ensure access to guidance, counselling and respite services.

Within this section of time poverty we should also consider those families that feel that they lack the skills or resources to adequately support their children, so therefore 'outsource' their childcare to providers to ensure that children are entertained, tutored and cared for. According to Travers (2024): 'Time poverty can lead to children feeling rushed, stressed and not listened to, thus not feeling supported, nurtured or valued' (Travers, 2024).

Let us at this point remember that only five years ago the entire world was in the middle of the largest global pandemic in recent history. Families all over the world were 'locked down', juggling a new way of 'normal' at home, while still working. For many, this was a time of joy and experiences together. But for many this was a time of great struggle.

Case Study: The Impact of Time Poverty During Covid-19

Grace, age 6, was an only child, the daughter of two consultants who worked in London hospitals – one parent worked with adults and the other with children. Grace's grandmother, who was also a nurse, supported childcare two days a week and her parents arranged their shifts to ensure she was dropped and collected by them the other three days. Prior to Covid-19, Grace rarely attended wrap-around provision and had a home life that was balanced and time spent each day with adults after school who had established a secure routine.

When Covid-19 hit, Grace's world was thrown upside down. Overnight she went from rarely attending childcare to being in full-time key worker provision and extended school. Grace found this very difficult as her friends were not in this provision and she was with children from other schools as well as her own. During this time Grace became withdrawn and tearful at drop-offs and collections. Grace found it hard to engage in the learning in the key worker provision and her behaviour became erratic. Her usual routine was completely changed due to her parents and grandmother working longer shifts and the concerns about spreading the virus. During this time Grace was considered to be suffering the effects of 'time poverty' as her parents and key carers did not have the time (and often emotional capacity) to support her in the same way as they had before Covid-19.

During this time, her school ensured that additional provision was provided for Grace within the school day, and Grace had additional support from the pastoral lead and her class teachers. They created family boxes, shared stories and spent time doing 'fun' activities that Grace was missing at home. Grace had specific times in the day when she shared stories with her parents over MS Teams in school to ensure that they had protected time when her parents had breaks and she felt connected.

Time poverty can have severe and far-reaching consequences, including lower self-esteem and wellbeing, reduced physical health and reduced attachments, to name a few. After life began to return to normal and her routine returned, Grace's behaviour began to settle down, and her family shared how thankful they were for the additional support during this period of insecurity. Poverty and disadvantage do not always last forever, but its impacts can, if they are not supported and recognised.

Case study question: How can schools recognise and respond to time poverty in families to protect children's emotional wellbeing and sense of security during periods of disruption?

Minority Groups

Childhood disadvantage disproportionately affects ethnic minority groups in the UK and is closely linked to lower income; material deprivation and experiences of racism, leading to significant but varied challenges in health, education and development. According to Madigan et al. (2023) many ethnic minority children are also exposed to higher levels of ACEs, including discrimination and poverty, alongside poorer housing conditions and environmental risks such as air pollution, which further affect wellbeing and development.

Additional challenges include limited access to timely family support services, disparities in parental engagement with early literacy and mental health inequalities, as minority children often receive lower quality and quantity of mental health support despite potentially greater need. However, cultural strengths, positive childhood experiences and strong family or community support can act as protective factors that buffer the effects of adversity, although this resilience may diminish in the context of sustained or severe disadvantage, highlighting the need for holistic, multi-sectoral approaches to address deep-rooted inequalities while recognising both risk and resilience within ethnic minority communities. This is becoming more prevalent in our schools. Statistics from World Data (2025) show that 16% of the UK population – which is approximately 10.7 million people – are from ethnic minority backgrounds (World Data, 2025). This will be evident in schools too.

Schools and settings can address this in a range of ways:

- Creating an inclusive school ethos where diversity is valued and respected.
- Diversifying the curriculum to reflect different cultures, histories and experiences.
- Providing targeted academic and language support, such as English as an Additional Language (EAL) programmes and mentoring.
- Building strong partnerships with parents, families and local communities.
- Closely monitoring pupil progress to identify and address gaps early.
- Ensuring staff are culturally competent and able to build trusting, supportive relationships with pupils.
- Actively addressing systemic barriers to achievement, including experiences of racism.
- Maintaining high expectations for all students through inclusive teaching practices.
- Supporting specific needs, such as language development, to improve educational outcomes for all pupils.

What is important to recognise is that this disadvantage can be temporary for some groups. When looking at attainment, overall data shows that some ethnic minority groups can overcome the initial disadvantage barriers and outperform disadvantaged white British pupils, particularly boys (Education Policy Institute, 2025).

When considering ethnic minority groups, it is important to recognise the presence of transient Traveller communities and to understand how they are integrated and supported within school settings. This includes both short-term support for families who are temporarily based in an area and longer-term strategies for more settled Traveller families, ensuring they are encouraged to attend school and fully engage in learning. Friends, Families and Travellers (2023) conducted research into the attendance and attainment of Traveller children in education. The research identified and explored some key barriers that this group of children have and possible solutions to overcome these barriers.

Some of the barriers that were identified in the report included:

- High rates of student dropout throughout secondary education, with figures unknown but estimated that around 50% of children do not transition to secondary school.
- Limited inclusive teaching that recognises and celebrates Gypsy, Traveller and Roma cultures and histories.
- Widespread bullying and discrimination faced by Gypsy, Roma and Traveller children.
- Digital exclusion, including limited access to devices or insufficient parental digital literacy, creating barriers to learning at home. Parents often have lower literacy levels and less ability to access learning. This was particularly evident during the pandemic (2020), when the attainment gap widened further.
- Inadequate support and systems to help travelling families access and sustain consistent education.

(Friends, Families and Travellers, 2023)

If you have children from the travelling community in your school it is important to consider how they are integrated, supported, seen and valued. Take a moment to consider this within the context of your school.

Language Barriers and Disadvantage

In the 2023/24 school year in England, around 1.7 million pupils - approximately 20.8% of the school population - spoke EAL, reflecting a continued increase in recent years (GOV.UK, 2024). The proportion of pupils recognised as having English as an additional language is currently higher in primary schools than in secondary schools, with the greatest concentration found in London and the West Midlands (GOV.UK). This growing and diverse population presents both opportunities and challenges for the education system, highlighting the need to understand the impact of language on learning, social integration and equitable access to educational outcomes.

Language barriers can create disadvantage at every stage of a child's educational journey. This form of disadvantage arises when pupils, parents and educators do not share a common language, limiting understanding, participation and parental engagement, while also negatively affecting academic progress. For pupils, language barriers can lead to difficulties in understanding lessons, following instructions and engaging with tasks, increasing the risk of falling behind academically. They may also experience reduced confidence in classroom participation due to fear of making mistakes, social isolation from peers and an increased cognitive load as they learn a new language alongside subject content.

It is essential to recognise that language barriers also affect families. Gaps in language proficiency can restrict parental involvement in school activities, limit understanding of a child's progress and reduce the ability to support learning at home, all of which can influence educational outcomes. Teachers, likewise, face challenges in addressing these barriers, often requiring specialised training and targeted strategies to support diverse learners, while communication difficulties can also arise between staff. Overall, language barriers impact learners from early years through to higher education, hindering social integration, educational attainment and equitable access to learning opportunities.

It is essential that teachers and practitioners are consciously considering strategies they can use to support children with English as an additional language within the classroom - many of these strategies also support children with speech and language difficulties and children with special education needs. Supporting EAL students effectively requires attention to the classroom environment, communication, instructional strategies, collaborative activities and home-school connections. Considering these areas, strategies and methods will help you increase engagement and attainment of this disadvantaged group of learners.

Area of Provision	*Strategies*	*Tips and Tricks*
Classroom environment and communication	Visuals and props, clear speech, strategic seating, extra processing time, positive reinforcement	• Visual timetables • Picture cards • Photos • Story props • Speak slowly, avoid idioms, use gestures • Seat near teacher or supportive peer • Allow 3-5 seconds for responses • Praise effort and small achievements
Instructional strategies	Pre-teach vocabulary, scaffolding tools, first language support (translanguaging), repetition and modelling, link to culture	• Introduce key words before lessons • Use sentence starters • Engage with vocabulary mats and knowledge organisers • Let students discuss ideas in home language first if possible with peers or staff • Repeat tasks and model clearly, with visuals if possible • Relate lessons to students' cultural backgrounds • Consider the use of translators to explain tasks where necessary
Activities and collaboration	Drama and role play, collaborative tasks, word work	• Act out scenarios for language practice • Pair with peers who can model language or share home language, even if this sometimes means working with students in different year groups • Focus on individual words or short phrases to build spoken and then written language skills
Home-school connection	Communicate with parents, send home resources	• Provide translated school information and visuals • Consider the use of Google Translate on newsletter and the school website to support parental engagement • Send vocabulary flashcards and simple games to reinforce learning at home • Consider community links with other families to support engagement at parents' evenings and school events

Figure 2.5 Supporting engagement for children and families with English as an additional language

(TICK Hub, 2026)

Special Education Needs

Children with Special Educational Needs and Disabilities (SEND) in England arguably face multiple layers of disadvantage that affect their social and academic outcomes.

Socially and emotionally, these children often experience bullying, friendship issues and difficulties forming connections in schools (Rowley, 2012). Academically, they may well face delayed identification of needs and missed early support which can widen attainment gaps and lower expectations in some schoolsb further limiting opportunities. Access and inclusion challenges are also significant, including difficulties receiving suitable support and securing specialist resources or funding. These challenges are often compounded by poverty, creating a term coined by the Sutton Trust 'double disadvantage' that exacerbates poorer outcomes (O'Regan and Latham, 2025).

Statistics from a UK Parliament research briefing (2025) states that approximately one in five pupils in England (19.6%-20.5%) have SEND, with over 1.7 million children receiving support in early 2025 - primarily through SEND support in schools or settings (around 14%) or Education, Health and Care Plans (EHCPs, around 5.3%) (Long, 2025).

Data from Sutton Trust (2025) reveals that the number of children identified with SEND has risen across all school types, and EHCPs have nearly doubled since 2016, from 2.7% to 5.2% in 2025. The disadvantage is further highlighted for children eligible for free school meals overrepresented in the SEND cohort. Data shows that 39.3% of those receiving SEND support and 43.8% of EHCP recipients are also eligible for free school meals, compared to 25.7% nationally (O'Regan and Latham, 2025).

Is This a Double Disadvantage?

This goes far deeper than the surface level with these socio-economic disparities being evident in parental access to special school places and formal diagnoses:

- 41% of middle-class parents secured a special school place for their child compared to 25% of working-class parents, and working-class parents are more likely to experience lengthy waits for SEND diagnoses.
- The legal timeframe in the UK for an EHCP assessment is 20 weeks, but in reality this is frequently exceeded, with an average wait of around 54 weeks due to funding and staffing shortages, particularly in educational psychology.
- Reports such as Double Disadvantage (Sutton Trust, 2025) highlight that children with SEND from low-income families face major inequalities in accessing much-needed support, a situation compounded further by where you live - for example, children from poorer families are more likely to receive support if they live in wealthier areas with higher expectations (O'Regan and Latham, 2025).

This all reveals the effects of family socio-economic status, the area in which you live and arguably the huge inequities in SEND provision.

Health and Hidden Disadvantage

The final disadvantage we would like to explore in this chapter is linked to health. We have discussed the importance of addressing education disadvantages for children with SEND, but let's finally consider health disadvantages. It is often hidden in terms of disadvantage but can also be very dangerous when it occurs. Not all disabilities are visible, and this is the same with disadvantage.

In the UK, schools are legally required under the Children and Families Act 2014 to support pupils with medical conditions, including allergies. This often involves creating Individual Healthcare Plans (IHPs) and Allergy Action Plans (AAPs) to ensure children can participate safely in school activities. Despite these measures, safety concerns, gaps in staff training and anxiety about managing allergic reactions frequently lead to school absences and, in some cases, consideration of home-schooling. As a result, attendance and inclusion are affected, with 70% of parents reporting that their allergic child has missed school due to their condition, often for medical appointments, health-related issues or anxiety (UK Parliament, 2025).

Research shows that food allergies in children are increasing, with approximately 1 in 13 children affected – nearly two children in every mainstream UK classroom. This prevalence has almost doubled over the past decade. In total, around 40% of British children have at least one allergy, and 1 in 100 children has a life-threatening allergy that could trigger anaphylaxis (Imperial Biomedical Research Centre, 2024).

Children spend a significant portion of their day at school – at least 20% of their time – and data indicate that 18% of food allergy reactions occur in school, with 25% of first-time anaphylactic reactions happening on school premises. In the UK alone, allergies are responsible for nearly half a million days of education lost each year (Imperial Biomedical Research Centre, 2024).

These statistics raise important questions about the impact of allergies on a child's learning and education. Evidence suggests that children are more likely to experience an anaphylactic reaction at school than at home, highlighting the critical role schools play in managing allergies (Jamjoom, Altirkistani and Baljoon, 2024). Headteachers, governors and school staff must acknowledge gaps in allergy management and take proactive steps to safeguard pupils, ensuring they can learn, participate and thrive safely.

To support children with allergies, it is essential that schools have a robust allergy policy that includes anaphylaxis. Addressing allergies as a disadvantage should be a whole-school approach, and every member of the school's community should be trained to understand the risk; how to reduce them and apply first aid to respond to an allergic reaction. It is essential that children with allergies feel included and awareness of this should be discreetly woven into school Personal Social Health and Economic (PSHE) schemes and day-to-day learning.

It is also important, as with medical care, that communication is clear and concise so all involved can address it and communication is open between everyone involved. Risk assessments should be in place and regularly addressed, and schools may consider the role of a 'Designated Allergy Lead' who would be responsible for ensuring that systems and processes are in place as well and liaising to ensure medication is up to date and available in the event of an emergency. This person could be responsible for supporting the development of an Anaphylaxis Emergency Response plan (see an example in our resources section) and schools may wish to consider practices of their anaphylaxis responses in the same way they practise a fire drill.

> I am delighted to hear of the launch of 'Allergy School', the new educational programme by The Natasha Allergy Research Foundation. Improving understanding of this issue is so important for keeping children with food allergies safe and ensuring they are able to participate fully in activities at school or in our wider communities. I am particularly heartened that my King's Foundation has been closely involved with the project, helping all of us to become more aware of the many ways we can support one another, especially the more vulnerable in our society.
>
> (King Charles on The Allergy School, Allergy Research Foundation, 2025)

On the Ground Running – You Cannot Be What You Do Not See

So as we reach the conclusion of this chapter we can take time to reflect on what we can do on ground level to support children in our schools and settings. We know that for many children and young people, their second chance in school is in fact their only chance to see and visualise their potential and be successful.

Take a moment to reflect on the children in your class or school who belong to the groups discussed throughout this chapter. These are not the typical pupils often labelled as disadvantaged, but they still face significant challenges.

Examples include:

- Children who are not eligible for pupil premium but experience financial hardship at home, limiting access to extra-curricular activities or social groups.
- Children with a family member who is seriously ill.
- Children who have not attended any pre-school or early education.
- Children who have a parent in prison.

How can we support these children in overcoming social, emotional and academic barriers? Can you identify a child in your class or school who falls into one of these categories? In what ways do their challenges differ from those of other pupils?

Now reflect on what strategies you, as a teacher, or your school have in place to identify and support these children. How are their progress and wellbeing tracked, and what measures exist to provide support both in the classroom and throughout school life? It is also important to consider what drives and motivates these children. What experiences and opportunities do the school offer them, and how are local resources being used to help broaden their horizons and expose them to the possibilities available in their community?

Jaywick Sands, Essex, is currently ranked number one in the 'Index of Multiple Deprivation' in England – a measure of extreme deprivation (GOV.UK, 2025). The Index of Multiple Deprivation is based on factors such as income, employment, education, health, crime and housing and compares the levels of deprivation across different areas and neighbourhoods in England.

Recent work with schools on the Essex coast, near Jaywick Sands, focuses on the theory 'that children cannot be what they cannot see' and also what they do not experience also impacts their life chances. Imagine looking at the windfarms along the Essex and Norfolk coast but never actually knowing what they are or why they are in fact there. If children are given the power of knowledge about jobs and sectors in their local area, they can see the opportunities available to them, on their doorstep.

When considering disadvantages and how to raise the barriers we can consider the trips and experiences that we offer children. When planning trips and experiences, it's important that children have their eyes opened to the world around them (such as the windfarms in Essex) to culture, literature, the arts, sport and, of course, joy! Consider how careers and enterprise are taught in school – do children have opportunities to meet ex-pupils who have been successful in the local labour market? Are pupils visiting universities and places of interest in their local vicinity? Do career days have representation from a range of jobs and speakers that represent the school?

Case Study: Curriculum Content

We recently worked with a Chelmsford primary school to revise their history/ geography curriculum to ensure it was reflective of the children in the cohort and their cultural background. As part of this they continued to learn about Earnest Shackleton and his explorations of the South Pole, but instead of then studying another dead white European male we adapted the planned to explore Namira Salim, a very much alive, female Pakistani polar explorer (as well as an astronaut and artist!). Considering the demographic makeup of the class was essential when planning this and ensuring engagement and representation. The school made contact with Namira Salim via social media, and she replied to the class answering their polar questions. At the end of the topic a parent of a girl of Pakistani heritage approached the school and thanked them for showing her daughter what she could be. The mother was quoted as saying: 'She loves space and snow but I am sure she could never imagine herself in either of those places – you have shown her that people like her are explorers and astronauts.' This is education for all.

Case study question: How does adapting curriculum content to reflect pupils' identities and lived experiences influence their sense of possibility, belonging and engagement with learning?

In conclusion, disadvantage cannot be neatly defined, and what we often see is only the tip of the iceberg. As educators, it is essential to take a broader view to address the full range of barriers faced by disadvantaged children.

Regardless of the challenges children encounter, it is vital that they are supported to process their emotions and gradually build resilience. This is a step-by-step process that cannot be rushed; without it, the barriers they face will remain in place. Schools and classrooms must be environments where all children – particularly those from disadvantaged backgrounds – feel safe, secure and valued. Only then can they begin to overcome obstacles, learn effectively, grow and thrive.

While it is impossible to identify every gap in a child's experiences, by widening our perspective, we can ensure that all pupils are nurtured and supported to strive and achieve, rather than merely survive, within education.

Chapter Takeaways

Reflections

- Disadvantage is highly complex with no one-size-fits-all.
- Disadvantage can affect anyone at any point for many different reasons, but poverty and additional needs are high indicators of disadvantage.
- Equality does not ensure that all children can meet their potential; children need equity – not all children need the same things to have their needs met and to prosper.

- Time poverty, health poverty and additional languages all impact disadvantage in pupils.

Now Consider

- Consider what disadvantaged looks like in your own locality.
- How do you support children's resilience?
- What steps do you actively take to promote growth mindset?
- How do you raise aspirations around careers and employment opportunities?

Enhanced Provision and Ideas to Support Learning

- Consider class passports so all adults know the different needs of each pupil – such as SEND, who uses fidget toys or has movement breaks, those that have specific seating places, hearing aids/ radio aids and other important information.
- Ensure all adults are aware of medical needs in the classroom.
- Consider how families are engaged in learning experiences – what works best for your community – during school hours/evenings? Online or face-to-face?
- Remember every day is a new day – reset, recharge and go again – sometimes you are the only safe space for a child.
- Record concerns on your school system – every small detail is a puzzle piece of a bigger picture.

Further Reading

- *Addressing educational disadvantage in schools and colleges* –Marc Rowland
- *Who am I teaching?* Poppy Gibson
- *Early childhood theories* – Aaron Bradbury and Ruth Swailes

Useful websites for further reference:

- https://www.littleparachutes.com/category/issues/parent-prison/
- https://www.prisonadvice.org.uk/get-help/children-young-people/supporting-your-child/
- https://childrenheardandseen.co.uk/what-we-offer/
- https://parents.actionforchildren.org.uk/home-family-life/family-relationships/supporting-a-child-with-a-family-member-in-prison/
- Supporting a child with a family member in prison: www.prisonreformtrust.org.uk

- National Information Centre on children of Offenders: https://www.nicco.org.uk/
- Barnardo's: https://www.barnardos.org.uk/get-support/support-for-parents-and-carers/children-with-a-parent-in-prison

Books and Resources to Support Children with a Parent or Relative in Prison:

- *My daddy's in jail* - Anthony Gurdid
- *Daddy's time out* - Rachel Nee Hall
- *The night Dad went to prison* - Melissa Higgins
- *Far apart, close to heart* - Becci Bertha
- *Tommy's dad* - Emma Randall-Caprez
- *My dad is in jail* - Amber Ryan
- *Kofi's mummy* - Richard Dyches
- *Someone I know lives in prison* - Rebecca Myers

Books About Parents Going Away (Work/Travel etc.):

- *My Daddy is going away* - McGregor and Yarlett
- *When Daddy travels for work* - Goeden
- *Mackey's monsters - when daddy works away* - Wildney
- *When Mum travels for work* - Goeden

Books Dealing with Death:

- *The invisible sting* - Patrice Karst
- *Grandpa's island* - Benji Davies
- *The brightest star* - Paul Wilkinson
- *Where did she go?* - Lloyd and Percival
- *Badger's parting gift* -Susan Varley
- *A shelter for sadness* - Anne Booth
- *It won't ever be the same* - Korie leigh

Bibliography

Asmussen, K., Fischer, F., Drayton, E. and McBride, T. (2020). 'Adverse childhood experiences: What we know, what we don't know, and what should happen next'. London: Early Intervention Foundation. https://www.eif.org.uk/report/adverse-childhood-experiences-what-we-know-what-we-dont-know-and-what-should-happen-next.

Barnardo's. (2026). *Young carers*. https://www.barnardos.org.uk/get-support/young-carers.

Benedict Blyth Foundation. (2023). 'React'. https://www.benedictblythe.com/wp-content/uploads/2024/03/BBF_React_LR.pdf.

Carers Trust. (2026). 'About young carers'. https://carers.org/about-caring/about-young-carers.

Department for Education. (6 June 2024). 'Schools, pupils and their characteristics, Academic year 2023/24'. Explore Education Statistics. https://explore-education-statistics.service.gov.uk/find-statistics/school-pupils-and-their-characteristics/2023-24.

Department for Education. (23 October 2025a). 'Cost of school uniforms'. London: Department for Education. https://www.gov.uk/government/publications/cost-of-school-uniforms/cost-of-school-uniforms.

Department for Education. (20 November 2025b). 'Free breakfast clubs: Guidance for schools on the early adopter programme, April 2025 to March 2026'. Department for Education. https://www.gov.uk/government/publications/free-breakfast-clubs-guidance-for-schools-and-trusts/free-breakfast-clubs-guidance-for-schools-on-the-early-adopter-programme-april-2025-to-march-2026.

Department for Education. (1 September 2025c). 'Keeping children safe in education 2025'. London: Department for Education. https://assets.publishing.service.gov.uk/media/68add931969253904d155860/Keeping_children_safe_in_education_from_1_September_2025.pdf.

Department for Education. (2025d). 'Pupil premium: allocations and conditions of grant 2025 to 2026'. London: Department for Education. https://www.gov.uk/government/publications/pupil-premium-allocations-and-conditions-of-grant-2025-to-2026.

Early Childhood Inequalities. (2022). 'Early childhood inequalities'. Institute of Fiscal Studies. https://ifs.org.uk/publications/early-childhood-inequalities-0.

Education Endowment Foundation. (2025). 'The EEF guide to the pupil premium'. London: Education Endowment Foundation. https://educationendowmentfoundation.org.uk/using-pupil-premium.

Education Policy Institute. (2025). 'Annual report'. Education Policy Institute. https://epi.org.uk/annual-report-2025/.

Forces Children's Education. (2026). 'Resources'. https://forceschildrenseducation.org.uk/resources.

Friends, Families and Travellers. (November 2023). 'Education inequalities facing Gypsies, Roma and Travellers in England'. https://www.gypsy-traveller.org/wp-content/uploads/2025/03/Education-inequalities-faced-by-Gypsies-Roma-and-Travellers-in-England-briefing-2.pdf.

GOV.UK. (17 November 2025). 'English indices of deprivation 2025: Statistical release'. https://www.gov.uk/government/statistics/english-indices-of-deprivation-2025/english-indices-of-deprivation-2025-statistical-release?utm_source=chatgpt.com.

Imperial Biomedical Research Centre. (2024). 'Food allergy continues to rise in the UK with many still left without treatment'. https://imperialbrc.nihr.ac.uk/2024/08/28/food-allergy-continues-to-rise-in-the-uk-with-many-still-left-without-treatment/?utm_source=chatgpt.com.

Jamjoom, M., Altirkistani, B. and Balijoon, J.M. (2024) 'School teachers' knowledge and attitudes related to anaphylactic relations: A cross-sectional study'. *Cureus*, 16(10). https://www.researchgate.net/publication/385202906_School_Teachers'_Knowledge_and_Attitudes_Related_to_Anaphylactic_Reactions_A_Cross-Sectional_Study.

Kalmijn, M. (2023). 'The association between parental separation at the school level and student outcomes in four European Countries'. Royal Netherlands Academy of Arts and Sciences. https://pure.knaw.nl/portal/en/publications/the-association-between-parental-separation-at-the-school-level-a/.

Long, R. (2025). 'Special Educational Needs: Support in England'. London: House of Commons Library. https://commonslibrary.parliament.uk/research-briefings/sn07020/.

The King's Foundation. (11 February 2025). 'The King's Foundation supports The Natasha Allergy Research Foundation to launch Allergy School'. https://kings-foundation.org/the-kings-foundation-supports-the-natasha-allergy-research-foundation-to-launch-allergy-school.

Madigan, S., Deneault, A.-A., Racine, N., Park, J., Thiemann, R. et al. (2023). 'Adverse childhood experiences: A meta-analysis of prevalence and moderators among half a million adults in 206 studies'. https://doi.org/10.17863/CAM.104322.

Murray, J. and Farrington, D.P. (2009). 'The effects of parental imprisonment on children', *Crime and Justice*, 37(1), 133–206.

National Governance Association. (January 2025). 'Disadvantage: Widening the lens'. NGA. https://www.nga.org.uk/news-views/directory/disadvantage-widening-the-lens/.

NICCO. (2026). National Information Centre on Children of Offenders. https://www.nicco.org.uk/.

OECD. (29 January 2025). 'Reducing inequalities by investing in early childhood education and care, starting strong'. *OECD*. https://www.oecd.org/en/publications/reducing-inequalities-by-investing-in-early-childhood-education-and-care_b78f8b25-en/full-report/mechanisms-behind-long-lasting-effects-of-early-childhood-education-and-care-policies_14351f70.html.

O'Regan, C. and Latham, K. (16 October 2025). 'Double disadvantage?' Sutton Trust. https://www.suttontrust.com/our-research/double-disadvantage/.

Prime Minister's Office. (2024). 'Plan for change'. https://www.gov.uk/government/publications/plan-for-change.

Rowley, E. (2012). *The educational experiences of Gypsy, Roma and Traveller children in schools.* London: The Children's Society.

TICK Hub. (2025). *Defining disadvantage*. Figure/infographic. London: TICK Hub.

TICK Hub. (2026). *The tip of the ACEs iceberg - What lies beneath?* Figure/infographic. London: TICK Hub.

Travers, M. (5 March 2024). 'A psychologist explains the concept of "time poverty" - and offers 4 fixes'. *Forbes.* https://www.forbes.com/sites/traversmark/2024/03/05/a-psychologist-explains-the-concept-of-time-poverty-and-offers-4-fixes/.

Trussell Trust. (2026). 'Ending hunger together' Trussell. https://www.trussell.org.uk/.

UK Parliament. (3 July 2025). 'Children with allergies: School safeguarding'. House of Commons debate. https://hansard.parliament.uk/commons/2025-07-03/debates/ACE98E5B-05C1-4D7A-BC82-8958FC345631/ChildrenWithAllergiesSchoolSafeguarding.

Winston's Wish. (2026). 'Childhood bereavement statistics for the UK'. Winston's Wish. https://winstonswish.org/about-us/facts-and-figures/.

World Data. (28 October 2025). 'British population by race 2025: Statistics & facts'. The World Data. https://theworlddata.com/british-population-by-race.

3

Unconscious Bias and the Impact of 'Short-Termism'

Consideration will be given to how we address unconscious bias and short-termism. We will dissect these barriers and the impacts they have, particularly on vulnerable and disadvantaged pupils. By considering what this might look like in our own schools or settings, we can begin to open doors for children that we did not know were closed before. In education, the real-life implications of implicit biases can create invisible barriers to opportunity and achievement for some students (and adults). Sometimes we are not even aware of the deep-rooted bias we have within us.

Pre-reading Reflection Questions

- What do you consider as a bias?
- How do we identify and build our own understanding of unconscious bias whilst understanding our own feelings and professional nature?
- Do you unconsciously link children because they are related? For example: 'Oh it's another Jones!'
- How do we ensure long-termism in a data-driven school system?

Unconscious Bias – What Does This Really Mean?

A definition of 'unconscious bias' offered by the Cambridge Dictionary: 'If you have an unconscious bias, you are not aware that you allow your personal opinions to influence your judgement so that you treat some people in an unfair way' (Cambridge Dictionary, n.d.).

As educationalists we like to consider ourselves as open-minded and non-judgemental. However, all humans have unconscious bias – things we are not aware of on the surface of our day-to-day life, and this is perfectly normal. It is how we address these biases and manage them that is important. Unconscious bias can influence a person's judgement without them even being aware of their judgement and subsequent actions. This could be how children are grouped in a classroom or who is picked to answer a question. It is widely known,

DOI: 10.4324/9781003624004-3

and well-documented in research, that teachers' *explicit* beliefs and expectations influence students' achievements (DeCuir-Gunby and Bindra, 2022).

Before we continue, let's take a moment to break down what could constitute an unconscious bias. An unconscious bias refers to a person's attitude, assumptions and beliefs that impact their actions or opinion without their conscious awareness. This could include a plethora of social or cultural biases including gender, age, weight, race, availability, beauty, among others. Some of these categories we will look at in more detail later in this chapter. It is important to remember that we are often unaware of these biases and, therefore, an unconscious bias can only begin to be lifted when more self-awareness is applied from individuals because they are generally well ingrained in a person's culture or personal views, perhaps over several years.

It's important to recognise that we are all affected by unconscious bias at some point in our lives, whether that is seen in the workplace or one's own home and social circles. The ability to distinguish friend from foe was an essential survival skill for early humans and this ability, in turn, quickly led to humans automatically categorising people according to their perceived characteristics. This is both a skill and flaw, but it is a fundamental quality of the human mind that helps provide some order to the complexities of life. Although we, as humans, like to think we are open-minded and objective, experience shows that this is not consistently the case. We are heavily influenced in ways that are completely separated from our conscious mind, and this impacts how we view people when we first meet. Perhaps consider now your initial thoughts on first meeting someone: what do you look for first? What is important for you?

Reflecting on this is important. Even Allerton et al. (2025) believe that having a strong awareness of unconscious bias is one of six signature traits of ethical leadership. They unpick four common types of bias that can affect the work culture in school: affinity bias, gender bias, overconfidence bias and confirmation bias.

In your role, take a moment at this point to consider and think more deeply about your own unconscious biases. This is something that we can find difficult as, by its very nature, we are often unaware of them so we need to take a step back and try to reflect on how others see us and how our subconscious actions can impact others.

Take a moment to consider the following statements in relation to your classroom, setting or school:

- *How do you seat the children?* Is this to do with behaviour? Friendships? Additional needs? Or are the children/students randomly placed? Do certain children always sit near you or at the back? How do adults in the classroom support the seating of children? Are children's abilities grouped in class or randomly grouped? Why did those groups get chosen in that way?

- *Do you always select the same children to volunteer?* Do the children with their hand up first always get to be the leaders? How are helpers selected? How is the star of the day or student of the term decided? Is this a group decision or an individual one?
- *In assemblies, do the same children and students always receive awards?* This is an interesting one to discuss – how are awards selected? Are they given at random and the most deserving child often gets more than others,or are they given and noted down so all children get the same? How do we build resilience as well as support all children to feel valued and celebrate their achievements? If the star reader is always the child who reads most at home does this really make them the star reader or is the parent/carer the actual star supporter? What about the child who reads independently three times a week at home, but reading is not valued or shared at home?
- *How do you select children for sporting/music and drama events?*
- *How do you group children in PE?*
- *Do you always send girls to wash their hands before the boys because they are quieter?*

Let's now consider some examples of unconscious bias in school settings and dig more deeply into the impact that this has in education; then we shall look into a child's wider life.

Bias and Boys – Boys Will Be Boys – Or Will They?

Some common unconscious biases are that boys will be boys, boys are more disruptive than girls, boys need to run about more and boys prefer learning outdoors. This is something that education has battled against for decades! We have all heard the many characterisations that boys are more disruptive and need to play more, whereas girls like to sit, write, draw and read; this is a common bias in life outside of school too, and it is a bias that is seen time again and one that schools are actively tackling. The unconscious bias one might hold that boys can't sit still and need to be more active than girls can then lead to gender bias (albeit unconsciously) that girls should do better in school than boys. We also hear that summer-born boys are less ready for school and need to play more. Could this then unconsciously mean teachers push girls in primary school more in the 'academic' subjects?

We know that at the end of the foundation stage girls outperform boys every year. In the academic year 2024/25, a higher percentage of girls, autumn-born children and children not eligible for free school meals had a good level of development when compared to boys, summer-born children and children eligible for free school meals, respectively.

So, if you are a summer-born boy, entitled to free school meals, then your chances of achieving the 'good level of development' are significantly lower than if you are an autumn-born girl who is not entitled to free school meals. Could this unconsciously influence a teacher's view of different children in the class? Could this impact who is in support groups because some children are 'more likely' to get to the expected level and thus impact data?

Characteristic	Characteristic type	2023/24	2024/25	Change (pp)
Sex	Female	75.0%	75.3%	0.3
	Male	60.7%	61.6%	0.9
	Difference (pp)	14.3	13.7	-0.6
First language	English	69.7%	69.9%	0.3
	Other than English	63.5%	64.7%	1.3
	Difference (pp)	6.2	5.2	-1.0
Free school meals	Not eligible	72.0%	72.5%	0.5
	Eligible	51.5%	51.3%	-0.3
	Difference (pp)	20.5	21.3	0.8
Term of birth	Autumn-born	75.6%	75.6%	-0.1
	Spring-born	69.5%	70.0%	0.5
	Summer-born	60.0%	61.1%	1.1
	Max difference (pp)	15.6	14.4	-1.1

Figure 3.1 Percentage of children with a good level of development by child characteristics (Department for Education, 2025)

The Lost Boys: How boys are falling behind in their early years, published by Save the Children (Read, 2016), discusses the theory that boys mature later than girls and suggests that entry into nursery, pre-school or formal education settings too early may place some boys at a disadvantage. This perspective, however, has been largely absent from contemporary evidence relating to the gender attainment gap. The report instead emphasises the importance of addressing the gender gap at an early stage, arguing that boys require not only equality in teaching and learning opportunities but equity through provision that meets their specific developmental needs. Without this, boys risk continued underachievement across their educational journey. Notably, the gender gap does not close at the end of the foundation stage but persists through to GCSEs, at the end of key stage 4. Recent data indicated that while the gap is narrowing, girls continue to outperform boys overall, with higher pass rates at grade 4 and above (approximately 70.2–73.6% compared with 64.3–67.5% for boys). In contrast, boys tend to outperform girls in mathematics, being more likely both to achieve a grade 4 or above and to secure the highest GCSE grades in this subject (Ofqual, 2025).

Last year, the Education Policy Institute highlighted that the attainment gap between girls and boys had narrowed since the pandemic (2020). However, this has to some extent been driven by falling attainment from girls, with analysis suggesting girls' performance has fallen since Covid-19. Some argue that this is linked to mental health, sleep issues and social media use, impacting concentration and exam performance, rather than boys actually doing better than girls (Hunt, 2025).

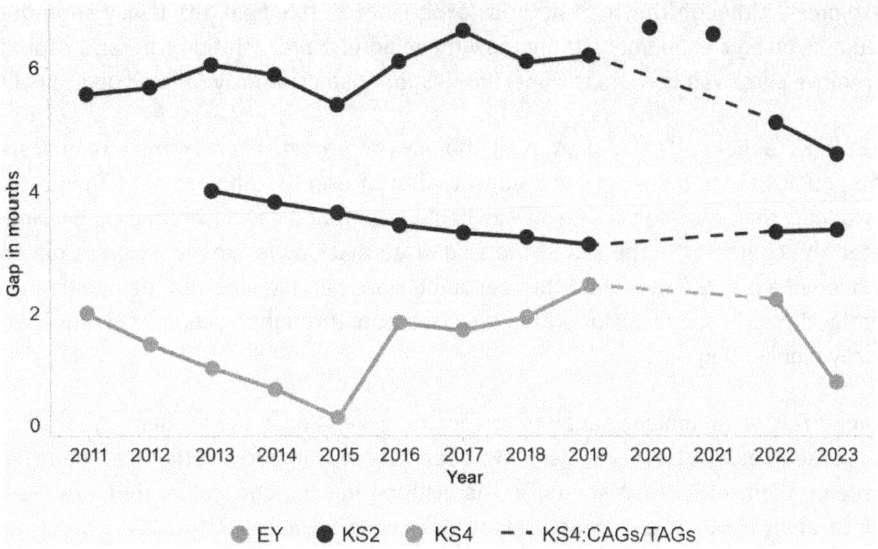

Figure 3.2 The gender gap between 2019 in key stages 2 and 4

(Education Policy Institute, 2024)

In data terms we can see there is narrowing of the gender gap, but boys are not closing that – this is being caused by a deterioration in girls' results rather boys achieving higher. So, in real-life terms are we doing enough to address this bias?

Cultural and Representational Bias

As teachers we should also consider our curriculum (this will be covered more in Chapter 8) and the adults that influence our children through our staff demographic and visitors.

Recently we supported a school to develop their curriculum. When we reviewed the curriculum, the school identified that in history and geography they taught about white, European explorers (most of whom were dead!). We then considered the school's changing demographic and the importance of representation. After completing this evaluation, they decided to continue to teach about the polar expeditions of Earnest Shackleton but to include another explorer as a contrast. It was identified that within the school community there were many families of Asian ancestry. Taking this into account and aiming to inspire girls too, the school chose the explorer Namira Salim. This approach introduced pupils to a range of contrasting explorers from both historical and contemporary contexts, representing different genders and cultural backgrounds, including European and non-European figures. At a parents' evening later in the year, a mother of Indian origin thanked the Year One teacher, explaining that her daughter now aspired to become an explorer. She shared that her child had thoroughly enjoyed the topic and had gone on to research it independently at home. The parents reflected that this was the first time their family had seen people like themselves represented as explorers. Although they had no prior experience in this field, the family subsequently joined a climbing club, demonstrating how meaningful representation can raise aspirations and remove perceived barriers to opportunities that had previously seemed unattainable.

The ELS (Essential Letters and Sounds) phonics programme is an example of inclusivity – in the phonics slides there are children who are represented who are in the minority. In a classroom recently, a phonics lesson was being taught and a child who wears hearing aids spotted the character in the slides and said, 'Hey that boy is like me – we are matching'. This opened a discussion around the reason he wore hearing aids and the opportunity for empathy, diversity and inclusion within the classroom through the choice of resources subliminally highlighting this.

It is important when looking ahead to forthcoming planning in the academic year that visitors or resources which are selected have been fully researched and that staff and children are seeing themselves represented in the visitors and the curriculum they are learning. Think carefully about what is beneficial for those children, in that school. Who do they need to hear speak? Which role models will be useful to them?

Consider:

- Are visits representing all children and opening their eyes to new opportunities and experiences? Are these visits challenging views and opening doors for equality, diversity and inclusion?
- Are there opportunities for different cultures to be shared and celebrated?
- Are visitors representative of a broad range of the school's community and the wider local demographic?
- What messages do the pupils in your school need to hear?

Poverty Bias

The disadvantage gap is widely recognised and remains persistently resistant to closure. Despite the introduction of the pupil premium in 2011, the attainment gap between advantaged and disadvantaged pupils continues to widen over the course of a pupil's educational journey and now stands at approximately 19.2 months by the end of secondary school. Education systems have long been shaped by institutional biases that disadvantage pupils from lower socio-economic backgrounds – barriers that schools and settings work relentlessly to dismantle. However, statutory assessments continue to reflect predominantly middle-class norms and experiences. For example, GCSE English writing papers frequently centre on themes such as travel, hotels or foreign holidays, experiences that some disadvantaged pupils may not have encountered and therefore struggle to relate to personally. These structural factors alone place working-class pupils at a disadvantage, even before considering additional barriers linked to lived experience, vocabulary exposure, access to books and learning resources, housing instability and health inequalities.

Case Study: Take a moment to consider these two pupils in a year 10 English class

Annabelle is from a middle-class family; both her parents are professionals and educated to degree level. She lives in a four-bedroom house with her family, where she has her own room to give her a quiet space and she has heating, hot water and electricity. She has an iPad of her own to do her homework on which is monitored, and time restrictions are in place to ensure she is sleeping and not online late at night. Annabelle went to a private day nursery and had some private speech and language interventions as a preschooler. Annabelle's parents read to her from birth and continue reading together, watching films and playing games. Annabelle has a healthy diet that consists of fresh food, and she takes part in two different sports clubs and a drama class. Annabelle is challenged to take risks and learn from her failures in a supportive environment. Her parents plan their work so she can take part in before- and after-school clubs and someone is around to help with her homework. Annabelle goes on two holidays each year and some of this is planned to be educational. She has travelled to Mexico and visited Chichen Itza after learning about the Mayans and has climbed the three peaks with her family. She has visited four continents and regularly goes to the theatre, day trips to London, the seaside and other cities and eats out in a range of different restaurants.

In contrast to Annabelle is Jack. Jack lives in a two-bedroom flat with his mum and his two younger brothers. Jack did not attend a pre-school and struggled with speech and language in school. He has some support from the local speech team in primary school, but this impacted his progress in phonics and thus other areas of the curriculum. Jack's mum works long hours, and he is often needed to help with childcare. He picks his youngest brother up from school and cooks dinner three times a week. Jack shares his room with his brothers and struggles to find a quiet space to study. Towards the end of the month there are the odd occasions when the electric metre runs out and there is no heating. Jack is sometimes late for school due to transport issues as he cannot always afford the bus, so he must walk (after dropping his brother to school). Jack has never played in a team outside of school, however he is a talented athlete. Jack has been to the seaside, the theatre and to London once on a school trip and has never been abroad.

Case study question: Now consider how equality of opportunities alone will not allow disadvantage barriers to be raised.

Special Education Needs and Unconscious Bias

Unconscious bias plays a significant role when addressing disadvantage for children with Special Educational Needs (SEN) by influencing educators to misinterpret students' behaviour, set lower expectations, misidentify needs and provide inconsistent support, which can result in poorer outcomes, increased segregation and disengagement.

Case Study: Unconscious Bias in SEND Education

Marie Saunders - Quadrant Outreach Lead - NE Essex

As educators we continually promote equality of opportunity, but our well-intentioned judgements can influence classroom practice, expectations and outcomes, including those in the areas of SEND, namely, those pupils with special needs and disabilities. In turn, our decisions are usually formed by the combination of interpreting information through our existing patterns of thought, reflecting on our personal experiences and the social context we are working in, all of which can constitute and contribute to unconscious bias.

Indeed, having taught in a special school setting where many pupils were non-verbal and presenting with significant cognition and learning needs, trying to be objective and advocate for those pupils is a clear example of where unconscious bias can unintentionally be present, as teachers endeavour to make decisions in the pupils' best interests. We also acknowledge that every single child has a unique biography, regardless of their cognitive level, any additional special needs and disabilities and whether they have been issued with an EHCP (Education, Health and Care Plan) or not in line with the SEND Code of Practice, 2014 which states:

> *'The four broad areas of need are set out within the SEND code of practice, which can be used as a basis for understanding and supporting a child's individual needs. You should not aim to fit the child strictly into the categories but should be flexible in understanding the whole child, using whichever parts of the different areas are relevant.' Excerpt from Help for Early Years Providers, 2025, DfE.*
>
> *[Accessed on 18 January 2026]*

In the UK, the four broad areas of need as outlined in the EHCP plan are Communication and Interaction, Cognition and Learning, Social, Emotional and Mental Health (SEMH), and Sensory and/or Physical Needs, as defined in the SEND Code of Practice, 2014. These areas frequently overlap when considering a child's special educational needs, and as educators we cannot pretend to be experts in these fields. When I led the whole school Mental Health initiative in a special school setting, we named it 'Creating Mental Wealth' to reflect that we are not mental health professionals and that all pupils can benefit from improved mental wealth, irrespective of their starting point.

Therefore, it is important that all teachers and educators be aware of unconscious bias when planning an in-school project, to ensure fairness and address inequalities and misconceptions, so that we do not predetermine expected outcomes and shape the project around these to ensure that the project meets these predetermined outcomes. Certainly, every pupil has a unique biography, and we need to be mindful that although some pupils may be categorised similarly in their EHCP plan, their presentation will also be unique as individuals.

I am using the example below of an SEMH focused project that I led in a mainstream junior school to illustrate how we addressed the issue of unconscious bias. Firstly, we considered the psychological mechanisms mentioned earlier, of awareness, motivation, individuation and empathy, to shape how we approached and planned the project. We agreed that the best way to do this was to capture the 'pupil voice' and let the pupils' responses be the driver for the project.

A whole-school project in response to pupil's SEMH needs in a mainstream junior school – using pupil voice to shape and drive the project

Below are the questions we asked the pupils, an analysis of their responses and details of the subsequent action plan that was put into place:

Following a discussion with the school and a climate walk involving the HT, SLT and SENCO, we identified the whole-school SEMH needs as the primary focus area due to the high level of local deprivation and pupil demographic, taking into consideration levels of pupil premium, free school meals, non-attendance and reduced timetables due to pupils SEMH needs.

As a starting point, we undertook a climate walk and were introduced to all the classes, taking this opportunity to ask these 'open' questions to capture 'pupil voice':

Pupil responses to the Year 3 class: What are the best things about your school

Pupil Responses	*Analysis – SEMH/ Curriculum Areas Recognised*	*Analysis – of SEMH Needs to Curriculum/ SDP and CPD*	*SLT Responses and Planning for 'evidence capture'*
Numeracy	Functional skills		
Literacy	Functional skills		
School dinners	Wellbeing – healthy living		

(Continued)

(Continued)

Pupil Responses	*Analysis - SEMH/ Curriculum Areas Recognised*	*Analysis - of SEMH Needs to Curriculum/ SDP and CPD*	*SLT Responses and Planning for 'evidence capture'*
Uniform	Sense of belonging/ community		
Teachers	Trusted relationships/ safe space		
Going outside	Physical/social and emotional wellbeing/ healthy living		

Pupil responses to the Year 6 class: What things can we do to make your school even better?

Pupil Responses	*Analysis - SEMH/ Curriculum Areas Recognised*	*Analysis - of SEMH Needs to Curriculum/ SDP and CPD and Potential Impact*	*SLT Response - Viability and Cost*	*Decision - Why*	*Timeframe - By Whom and By When?*
Basketball hoops outside	Physical wellbeing				
Football nets outside	Physical wellbeing				
Pretend play activities such as food and money	Functional/ life skills - imaginative play and role play activities				
Clubs	Social/ emotional wellbeing				

(Continued)

(Continued)

Uno Club	Social/ emotional wellbeing				
Science Equipment	Special interests				
Chess Club	Social/ emotional wellbeing - intellectual stimulation and challenge				
Every other week having a hot chocolate and chocolate biscuit	Special treat/ emotional wellbeing - recognition of success and 'just being'/ work-life balance				

Post-analysis discussion points and next steps included:

By the Year 3 class: What are the best things about your school?

Discuss the significance of the areas not mentioned

- *Creative activities e.g. art, music and interests linked to developing hobbies;*
- *Trips - wider life experiences;*
- *Careers/life skills - future aspirations.*

Celebrating the existing strengths to showcase 'What are the best things about your school?'

How: *Through the pupil lens-evidence capture the Year 3 pupil voice across the school using photographs of learning, activities and their lived experiences in school.*

By: *Staff to support and oversee the pupils planning, filming and interviewing peers and staff on their views and how these aspects of the school make them feel. That is, photographs, interview, podcast or short film. This genre will provide opportunities for pupils to develop their literacy and IT skills, be creative and experience different career/job roles, that is, writer, cameraman, interviewer,* *editor and producer. Photographs can be displayed with pupils developing their artwork displays. So, all three areas not mentioned (listed above) by the pupils can be explored during the evidence capture process and in a context that they are comfortable and familiar with.*

Next Steps: Link with SDP and the wider curriculum provision

By the Year 6 class: What things can we do to make your school even better?

1. ***Discuss the significance of the areas mentioned and not mentioned***
Mentioned:

- *Physical wellbeing – developing outside activities available;*
- *Life skills – using role play, i.e. food and money to promote understanding and independence skills around food, nutrition, cooking, managing money and budgeting;*
- *Clubs and special interests – celebrating pupil difference through club interests and social interactions;*
- *Special treat/celebrating success – developing self-worth, the value of effort, focus and success over time.*

Not mentioned:

- *Creative activities e.g. art, music and interests linked to developing hobbies;*
- *Trips – wider life experiences;*
- *Careers/life skills – future aspirations.*

2. ***Planning for change***

Involve the pupils in planning and leading on costing and purchasing the outside equipment – experiencing using money budgeting and careers – a caretaker role.

School to explore training staff and introducing the OPAL project to introduce more structured child-led outside play-based activities in school.*

Involve the pupils in planning, promoting and running their individual lunchtime clubs – with the School Council.

Involve the pupils in planning and setting up a chess club.

Survey pupils about their career/job knowledge. What jobs are out there, and the skills sets required for different jobs, i.e. inside, outside, practical skills, knowledge based, etc.

Plan visits to settings, i.e. zookeeper for a day and arrange visits to the school for pupils to meet people employed in different roles, e.g. fire fighter, vet, gardener, carpenter. Pupils to make suggestions around their interests to link initial visits with these.

SLT to evaluate these responses and review progress half termly with the School Council.

3. ***Next steps: Link with SDP and the wider curriculum provision***

** The OPAL Primary Programme blends elements of strategic school improvement practice, action planning, self-evaluation, playwork skills and knowledge, and 20 years of action-research.*

It is a mentor-supported school improvement programme addressing all 18 areas a school must plan for if they want to sustainably improve the quality of play with schools creating a personalised 18-month action plan for better play.

https://outdoorplayandlearning.org.uk/opal-programme/introduction/ [Accessed on 18 January 2026]

To conclude, we all agreed that as teachers and educators the project would have looked very different had we based it solely on our well-intentioned judgements without capturing 'pupil voice' and, by doing so, gained pupil buy-in from the outset, as they were instrumental to the project's design, planning, implementation and reviews. And finally, we anticipate the project to continue evolving and be responsive over time as the pupils' needs change and that it will have a greater impact than we first expected as the project has the potential to involve and thus improve the SEMH, wellbeing and mental wealth of every pupil in the school.

Case study question: Now think about how the SEND White Paper (2026) will impact provision in your school.

Bias and Privilege Opposed to Poverty

So far in this chapter we have looked at unconscious bias in relation to 'classic' disadvantage – SEND, poverty, culture and gender – but what if we flip the rhetoric and explore this from the other side. There is an assumption that children from affluent families are not disadvantaged or that children who attend private schools are more advantaged than those who go to comprehensives. Although the data clearly shows that attainment is higher at GCSE, is this a true reflection on disadvantage?

Let's now consider some of the unconscious biases that surround privilege. There is an assumption that all children in private education are from affluent families. That they all live in large houses and travel expensively. While this may be the case for some families, it is not reflective of *all* families. For some, private education is achievable through bursaries, through scholarships or through grants due to work (for example children of Armed Forces families).

Centre type	Percentage of results at grade 7 and above	Percentage of results at grade 4 and above
Academies	19.5%	68.1%
Free schools	23.7%	70.9%
Further education establishment	0.8%	18.0%
Secondary comprehensive or middle school	19.7%	68.5%
Secondary modern school/high school	12.9%	60.5%
Secondary selective school	63.2%	97.4%
Sixth form college	2.8%	29.0%
All state-funded	20.7%	66.5%
Independent school including city training colleges (CTCs)	48.1%	89.6%

Figure 3.3 Percentage of GCSE results at Grade 7 and above and Grade 4 and above by centre type, all subjects combined

(Ofqual, 2025)

While these children can access private education, there can be unconscious bias surrounding them. There is the assumption that they cannot afford all the trips, or the assumption that they can and should be accessing all trips and extra-curricular activities which their peers access, but this is not always financially viable. Over the past year, private schools distributed £1.1 billion worth of scholarships and bursaries to 156,000 pupils – that's about 30% of all children in private schools, highlighting that not all 'advantaged' children are as advantaged as others (Good Schools Guide, 2025). There is a sliding scale of bursaries, and in recent years these bursaries have been essential for professional families, as well as lower income families, with doctors, teachers and civil servants – who were once the backbone of many fee-paying school communities – more recently priced out without bursaries due to the cost of living.

The Royal National Children's Springboard Foundation supports schools with the allocation of their fully funded bursaries used in the placements for children facing barriers to opportunities and focus on attachment aware, trauma-informed practices to support wellbeing and educational opportunities.

Next, let's explore serving or ex-forces families. These children could technically be advantaged due to their education in private schools. However, alongside this there is a wealth of research around attachment, abandonment and trauma. Imagine being 8 years old and dropped off at an unfamiliar school with unfamiliar people and expected to thrive immediately. Children in this situation often live in a fight or flight mode. On paper they have wonderful experiences travelling the world and a great education but in practice they are forced to grow up independently without the same levels of nurture as a child in a family home. For Armed Forces families there is also the constant underlying risk of bereavement when a family member is on active duty.

There is also a third group of children who are considered privileged – those from wealthy backgrounds. While these children often benefit from significant material and educational advantages, they can also face distinct and often overlooked barriers. Unconscious biases within their social environments may influence their emotional development and their capacity to form secure, meaningful relationships in adulthood. For some young children, there is a tension in understanding: they may perceive themselves as fortunate to attend an expensive school and to have families investing heavily in their education yet simultaneously struggle to reconcile this with being separated from their caregivers. This dissonance can give rise to emotional attachment difficulties, fears of abandonment and experiences of trauma associated with disrupted relationships and loss of connection (Duffell and Bassett, 2016).

While children from more affluent families affront many privileges, there are still times when they could be considered disadvantaged. It's often assumed that they have time and presence, but in reality this is an unconscious bias and they are 'time poor'. They are often hothoused from club to club, in wraparound care and holiday clubs. At these times the bias is that these children are advantaged to do all the extra-curricular activities they take part in but for some, what they need is time and attachment. For some children, all the extras are too much and their bucket is full from a full day of school – this in turn can affect behaviour at home and in school. Consider 'time poverty' for a moment and the impact this has.

A child in a foundation stage class comes from a family where both parents have professional, challenging jobs, they attend breakfast, after-school club and holiday clubs. The parents do not always have time to read bedtime stories, bake cookies or ensure that emotional needs are met. They appear to be in a rush at drop-offs and often do not hug the child goodbye. At pick-up time the child is the last to leave and the parent collecting appears stressed and is often on the phone. At the start of the week this child can self-regulate and learn, but by the middle of the week they become emotional and struggle to manage their emotions. On the flip side the child takes three overseas holidays each year including a ski trip, they wear expensive clothes, they go to the theatre and take day trips with grandparents in the school holidays.

On the surface, we assume this child is not disadvantaged but this is an unconscious bias because disadvantage has not set boundaries.

Why does this matter? Because if we genuinely aim to educate the children and young people in our care, we must first seek to understand them in their entirety. Effective education begins with recognising pupils not simply as learners, but as human beings shaped by their experiences, relationships and emotional worlds. A holistic understanding is therefore essential to meeting their needs and enabling them to thrive.

Unconscious Bias, Girls and Sport

Women in Sport highlights that participation in competitive sport builds resilience, courage and self-belief in girls and young women, yet gender stereotypes and bias continue to limit the participation and confidence of young women in sport; which can have longer-term impacts on health and confidence in adult life. Research shows that only 49% of girls aged 5–11 take part in team sports compared with 70% of boys, and while 69% of girls in primary school rate their self-belief as good or very good, this still falls behind boys at 79% (Youth Sport Trust, 2026).

These gender gaps are reinforced by societal messages suggesting that girls are less competitive, that sport matters less for them or that it conflicts with femininity, a belief reflected in the fact that only 30% of parents see sport as very important for their daughters compared with 41% for sons. Schools can unintentionally reinforce this unconscious bias through the prioritisation of boys' competition, clubs, participation, opportunities and achievements. Alongside this, if not well managed, playgrounds are often dominated by boys' games such as football and basketball with girls' sports being sidelined. Take a moment to consider your playground.

Figure 3.4 Youth football coaching session demonstrating inclusive sport education

(Licensed image from Wix, February 2026)

In the 21st century this is a huge concern. We are all aware of the importance of physical activity for both physical and mental wellbeing, and it is well-evidenced that there are a wide range of physical, mental, academic and social benefits of participation in sport. These range from preventing conditions such as obesity and type-2 diabetes to supporting focus, engagement and thus impacting overall learning outcomes, wellbeing and, in the longer term, opportunities for future employment.

Barriers are not just in primary schools. They persist, and in fact are exacerbated, in adolescence. The Youth Sport Trust research (2026) shows that 64% of girls drop out of sport by age 16, a third citing unsuitable sports kit and many feeling uncomfortable with communal changing rooms as factors that impact on this. So, in education we must consider how this is addressed. How are sports kit designed? Does pupil voice play an active role in the design of kit? How is changing managed in both primary and secondary education to provide girls with a safe place they can change in private without being conscious of others around them?

However, there are signs of progress: inspired by the Lionesses' historic win in 2025. nearly 70% of 'sporty' girls now dream of reaching the top in sport, close to boys at 75%, and up from 50% just two years ago (Youth Sport Trust, 2026). Girls are also calling for greater gender equality, including equal media coverage, increased support for women's teams, stronger celebration of women's achievements, greater diversity among female role models and the eradication of the gender pay gap.

> Understanding unconscious bias doesn't mean you're cured of it. It means you're aware of how it operates and that awareness is the first step toward accountability. Bias influences who we trust, who we listen to and how we treat others. Left unchecked, it reinforces inequality. But when we recognize it, we can begin to challenge it - and choose to act differently.
>
> (Ineke Houtenbos, senior trainer with the NSPCC)

How can we address our own unconscious bias and those that are present in our schools?

Whole-school practices

- **Staff training (CPD):** Make sure staff understand unconscious bias, the backgrounds of pupils and the barriers some learners face.
- **Curriculum:** Ensure the curriculum reflects pupils' lives and includes a range of role models, including working-class voices.
- **Assessment and grading:** Use clear, fair systems for marking and moderation to reduce the impact of unconscious bias.
- **Using data:** Check whether disadvantaged pupils are underrepresented or making less progress. Learn from teachers who are successful and share good practice.
- **High expectations:** Hold the same high expectations for all pupils, regardless of background.

- **Relationships and culture:** Build strong relationships with pupils and families, and challenge stereotypes whenever they appear.

Personal classroom practices

- **Get to know your pupils:** Strong relationships help reduce assumptions and allow teachers to respond better to individual needs.
- **Reflect on your practice:** Notice who you question, praise or support most. Are all pupils getting equal attention?
- **Fair classroom strategies:** Use techniques that encourage everyone to participate and mix pupils by ability and background when working in groups.
- **Be consistent:** Apply rules and expectations fairly to all pupils, not just those you find easier to teach.
- **Consider your classroom:** Where do you stand when teaching? Who do you ask when questioning? Do you gravitate towards certain children? Who works with each group of children? Do the most disadvantaged pupils have the best teaching to ensure equity?

Take some time in your classroom to reflect on this or consider discussing this with your school team. Consider filming your own teaching.

- Do you stand in a particular spot?
- Do you tend to ask certain children?
- Are there children who cannot see you as clearly in the room?
- Do you tend to gravitate towards particular children or groups of children?
- Who are the additional adults in your classroom working with?
- How do you manage behaviour - does it differ with different groups or individuals?
- Do you understand the individual needs of each child - consider a class passport for cover staff to ensure a smooth transition of staffing.
- How do you model vocabulary to all children to ensure progression?

Short-Termism

In education the term short-termism refers to a teacher's or school's focus being on short-term goals and the result of these at the expense of the longer-term outcomes for pupils. This means that a key stage or year group fo cuses on the outcomes for that year without considering the longer-term issues that could arise. A child could be taught enough phonics to pass the phonics test in year 1 but longer term if they do not understand the purpose of the learning, they will fall short later in their education journey. Long-termism considers the outcomes for a pupil up to 10 years or more in the future based on their decisions at a set time. One might like to ponder the question: what is the point of school? Or education? Is it to achieve the highest SATs for the school? Is it to achieve a certain percentage of GCSE results? We know that there is a huge amount of pressure on schools to perform. Surely, the real measure of a school's success is what the students go on to do - long after their education has finished.

Consider a child who attends an intervention group in key stage 1 but is seemingly not making much progress. When we think short term, we are likely to remove the child from the intervention as it is 'not working' or there are other children who would seemingly benefit more but by doing this we have viewed only the short-term outcome. This action potentially ignores a host of future outcomes that could be more impactful on a child's life outcomes. Think of the hare and the tortoise. Sometimes slow and steady is more important than racing. If a child continues in an intervention making slow but steady progress perhaps in the long term we, as schools and teachers, have increased their life chances - their chance of passing the GCSE in that subject, that confidence that they have gained, how that impacts self-esteem and confidence and even the longer-term opportunities to access college and employment.

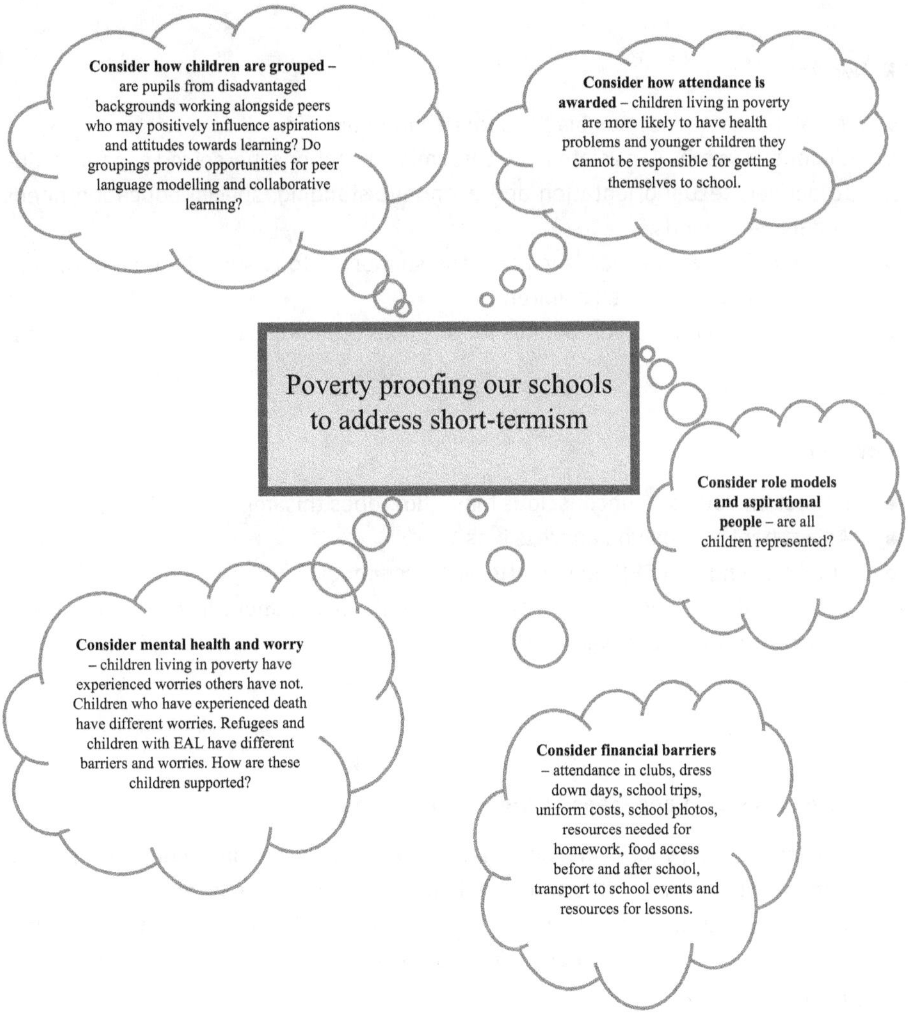

Figure 3.5 Ideas to address short terminism

(TICK Hub, 2026)

When we are considering short-termism, it is essential that we are looking at all areas of a pupil's school life and how missed opportunities in school can impact later life chances and opportunities. Long-term goals, high expectations and the inclusion of pupil voice are essential when we are considering poverty-proofing our schools and addressing unconscious bias and short-termism.

Let's consider some key areas we need to address when poverty-proofing our schools and addressing short-termism.

Chapter Takeaways

Reflections

- We all have unconscious bias at some point in our life.
- Unconscious bias can relate to cultural misconceptions, perceived capability due to gender, sexual orientation and economic standing, special education needs and medical needs.
- Consider how all staff are included and supported to ensure the best outcomes and opportunities for all children.
- Failing to plan for all eventualities for all pupils is planning for failure in the longer term.

Now Consider

- Reflect on your own unconscious bias - how does this impact you?
- As a school how do you address bias?
- What training and CPD do you offer in your school?
- Consider the resources in this chapter when thinking about how to make school even better for your pupils.

Enhanced Provision and Ideas to Support Learning

- Consider filming your own teaching to allow you to reflect on unconscious biases.
- Remember to consider the whole child not just the surface level.
- Consider programmes to help equity - The Literacy Trust - The Letter Box Club.
- Consider reviewing your curriculum to ensure representation of all pupils and staff.
- Explore ways pupils can be represented in the displays and artwork around the school.

Books for Supporting Children

- *The kids' book about diversity* - Charnaie Gordon
- *People need people* - Benjamin Zephaniah
- *The same but different* - Molly Potter
- *What if?* - Steve L Robbins
- *The proudest blue* - Ibtijah Muhammad
- *The other side* - Jacqueline Woodson
- *The wall in the middle of the book* - Jon Agee

Bibliography

Allerton, D., Mortuza, Y., Andrews, H., Knowles, R. and Parry, V. (2025). 'Tackling unconscious bias at personal and staff level is an essential ingredient of ethical leadership'. *Impact*, 23, 69-72.

Cambridge Dictionary. (n.d.) https://dictionary.cambridge.org/dictionary/english/unconscious-bias.

DeCuir-Gunby, J. and Bindra, V. (2022). 'How does teacher bias influence students? An introduction to the special issue on teachers' implicit attitudes, instructional practices, and student outcomes'. *Learning and Instruction*, 78, 101523.

Department for Education. (27 November 2025). 'Early years foundation stage profile results'. GOV.UK. https://explore-education-statistics.service.gov.uk/find-statistics/early-years-foundation-stage-profile-results/2024-25.

Duffell, N. and Basset, T. (2016). *Trauma, abandonment and privilege: A guide to therapeutic work with boarding school survivors*. London: Routledge.

Education Policy Institute. (2024). 'Gender'. Education Policy Institute. https://epi.org.uk/annual-report-2024-gender-2/.

Jiménez, E., Tuckett, S., Hunt, E. and Robinson, D. (17 March 2025). 'Breaking down the gap'. Education Policy Institute. https://epi.org.uk/publications-and-research/breaking-down-the-gap/.

Ofqual. (14 August 2025). 'Qualification results in England: Summer 2025'. GOV.UK. https://www.gov.uk/government/publications/qualification-results-in-england-summer-2025.

Read, C. (2016). 'The lost boys: How boys are falling behind in their early years'. Save the Children. https://resourcecentre.savethechildren.net/document/lost-boys-how-boys-are-falling-behind-their-early-years.

The Good Schools Guide. (2 December 2025). 'Who really gets private school bursaries - and should you apply?' https://www.goodschoolsguide.co.uk/uk-schools/advice/can-my-family-get-a-private-school-bursary.

Youth Sport Trust. (2026). 'Girls active: Closing the gender participation gap in sport'. Loughborough: Youth Sport Trust. https://www.youthsporttrust.org/programmes/targeted-interventions/girls-active.

4

A Culture of Inclusion

A culture of inclusion is a culture that supports and respects each and every individual. When considering inclusion, we must be open to all areas of inclusion and be aware that at times this could make us feel uncomfortable and push our own boundaries but it's important that we do this to ensure that all children have a 'second first chance'.

Pre-reading Reflection Questions

- How is your classroom and school inclusive?
- Have you considered the barriers that children face?
- How do you engage with families?
- Do you consider potential barriers that parents/carers might face?

A culture of inclusion is a culture that supports and respects all who are in the education setting. In order to truly support *all* children, teachers need to know their students. Creating an inclusive environment where all children can thrive simply does not happen by chance, it occurs through purposeful design. Research carried out by Greany et al., 2023 reveals that young people in inclusive settings and especially those from disadvantaged backgrounds do achieve well and have better outcomes. The research, which focused on secondary schools, showed that there is no 'one best way' to achieve inclusion but that the schools who do cater for the range of needs well adopt an 'inclusion for all' approach. The six schools which the research centred around showed certain core values but the main value was the quality of 'relationships'. By focusing on relationships, the schools created a strong sense of *belonging* - where the students were seen, known and cared for. The most important point here is that teachers *know* the students. These schools did not just treat each pupil equally; they recognised that some students needed different treatment and opportunities.

The values which shone through in these schools created a community of belonging. Students were known, cared for, understood and supported in ways that met their particular needs and ultimately, inclusion was the outcome.

DOI: 10.4324/9781003624004-4

Figure 4.1 A sense of belonging

(Adobe Stock, 2024. Licensed stock photograph. Used with permission)

What can we learn from this study? When schools look to address inclusion, it is an immersive and whole-school approach where every pupil, member of staff and member of the school community is not just *in* the school, they are *part* of the school. It is where all children, regardless of their start in life, have the same opportunities as their peers to benefit from the highest quality teaching and experiences the school can provide – essentially equity is the guiding principle. This needs to be a conscious effort, because there are some decisions that run the risk of making the situation worse for an already 'disadvantaged' pupil. Rowland (2021) identifies four core elements for the successful implementation of inclusion. We have adapted these to:

- Relationships
- Skills for life
- Social, emotional and mental health
- Oracy and vocabulary

Let us first consider what inclusion looks like in school. First ask yourself these questions:

- How well do you know each child?
- What do you know about each child's life outside of school?
- Do you know what their barriers are in terms of accessing school life to the full?
- Do you know what they really enjoy and what their passions are?
- Are you aware of any 'hidden' children in your school whose background you are not clear on?
- What are your own relationships like with the students you teach?

Now consider the implications if you *don't* know the answers to these questions. The Education Endowment Foundation (2025b), in their recent guidance on how to implement the pupil premium strategy, advises that 'It's important to know and understand your whole-school context - including individual pupil and family needs' (Education Endowment Foundation). The main point they are suggesting is that schools must regard the pupil premium strategy as a long-term strategy, rather than a one-off task. Likewise, the House of Commons Education Select Committee have recommended that Children's Wellbeing and Schools Bill (2025) should be used to implement automatic enrolment in the eligibility checks for free school meals - ensuring better coverage, especially in younger children. If we are to truly cater to the needs of the young people in our schools, it goes without saying that we need to have a well-rounded understanding of their backgrounds.

Knowing our students is important. We know that the register of children in receipt of the pupil premium funding by no means shows the true picture of deprivation, poverty and the barriers that some children face to their learning. Therefore, being 'disadvantaged' is a much broader term.

Consider these statistics:

At the SecEd National Pupil Premium Conference (March 2025) it was highlighted that 'around 4.3 million children in the UK are living in poverty, yet only around 2.1 million are receiving free school meals'. This figure equates to around 32% of children who are living in poverty and are not receiving free school meals. A child is in poverty 'if their household income is below 60% of the national average (median) income' ('What is poverty?').

But there are other factors which need consideration. For example, the criteria for free school meals does not take into account factors such as housing costs and family size which are highly associated with poverty. It is also important that we consider the demographic makeup of our students as a way of identifying those who may well need support to ensure inclusion in all activities but that are the 'hidden cusp children' in terms of how we identify them for funding.

When thinking about identifying these *hidden* children within a class, it's important to remember that in the UK alone, statistics linked to those children living in poverty identified that 69% of poor children lived in working families and that 46% of children in families with three or more children were in poverty (Child Poverty Action Group, 2025). It also identified that 44% of children in lone parent families live in poverty and that 34% of children living in families where someone has a disability are living in poverty (Child Poverty Action Group, 2025).

The trajectory of the statistics continues. According to the Poverty Strategy Commission (2025), 'more than one third of children (36%) are living in families who are in deep poverty'. These are extremely depressing statistics.

What do they reveal? They highlight that poverty is not just about unemployment, but poverty is about other inequalities such as low wages, high costs and family circumstances. We can say that being employed does not guarantee security, family size really does matter, and the Early Years can be a vulnerable stage and having a disability increases disadvantage risks. As Cameron (2025) notes, 'Child poverty currently affects almost one in three children in the UK. Rates are higher among larger families, lone parents, Black and Asian households, and those raising a child with disabilities, as well as in some locations such as parts of London, where the figure rises above 40%.'

Let's explore this:

A study carried out at the Bradford Institute of Health Research has focused on addressing early life health and wellbeing to help reduce inequalities for children growing up in cities. The study, which was carried out over a five-year period (2019–2025), focused on the current life and prospects of children growing up in inner-city areas in England. Concluding findings found that 'there are many overlapping dimensions at play' (Cameron, 2025, p. 28):

- Families can be suddenly tipped into poverty, whether by illness, accidents or economic shocks such as Covid-19.
- Homes in need of retrofitting and upgrading impact mental and physical health.
- Lack of space to play, broken lifts and unsafe communal areas restrict children's everyday freedoms, impacting their health and development.
- In some cases, families experience high levels of loneliness, though the social support offered through community and faith networks can ease this.

Certainly, children's wellbeing and mental health have been reported on for some time now. In 2023, the Children's Society found that the mean score for happiness overall was lower than in the previous ten years. The results showed that children's happiness with friends, appearance, school and schoolwork had declined (The Children's Society, 2023). The findings in the report revealed that girls are particularly affected and were unhappy with their life as a whole (The Children's Society). The survey completed by 250 children and young people highlighted how important relationships are, in particular, having dependable and trusting relationships with those who care for them is crucial for feeling well and happy. The second factor revealed that happiness is strongly linked with having plenty to do – especially in the outdoors. Third was having agency – young people feel strongly that being able to make their own decisions and have a say over their life is important (The Children's Society, 2023).

The research highlights that wellbeing, family dynamics, cultural expectation and daily practicalities are the bedrock of academic performance. We need to ask questions, make no assumptions and explore every barrier before we intervene as educators.

Knowing Your Pupils

Knowing your students needs to be a priority. Clearly, deciding what data to collect on children and then collating this information is a time-consuming task. This is more than just numerical data; this is collecting information holistically about the pupils. There is always a wealth of quantitative data on children, but this is not the conclusion, this is just the starting point. Schools all have some sort of tracking system, which tells us exactly who is on track or not, but we need different layers of 'data'. As we have seen within this chapter so far, knowing who is in receipt of free school meals tells us some information, but not everything.

Interestingly, Rowland (2025) believes there is 'little difference between schools over what the pupil premium funding is spent on' for the pupil premium grant. Rowland emphasises the point that schools must consider their pupil premium approach and look at whether it is evidence informed, right for the setting and feasible to implement. Essentially, schools need to poverty-proof their school day. It is essential that all staff understand what inclusion and disadvantage truly are, the impact they can have on students and the signs teachers should be looking out for. Certainly, we have to go further than simply collecting data on students. In order to fully teach the whole child, teachers need to understand how that particular disadvantage is showing up in the pupil.

Potential Barriers

There are of course other factors to consider. Let's also think about inclusion in terms of ethnicity: 47% of children in Asian and British Asian families are living in poverty, 51% of children in Black/African/Caribbean and Black British families and around 24% of children in white families live in poverty (Child Poverty Action Group, 2025).

We also need to consider that groups of lowest-achieving children in each key stage - white British boys from low-income backgrounds have the lowest outcomes of any major ethnic group (Strand, 2021). This is a trend that begins early and persists through education and into adulthood.

By identifying potential barriers to inclusion, we can ensure that inclusion is not just a word schools use but something that is embedded in their make up; something that is not just talked about, but is accessible for every child, ensuring that every child feels a true sense of belonging where they can be themselves, be part of every opportunity they wish to access and be prepared to be part of an ever-changing, diverse and interconnected world.

To summarise so far:

We need to know the whole picture when considering the young people we are working with - some concerning statistics to highlight:

- 69% of poor children lived in working families;
- 46% of children in families with three or more children were in poverty;
- 44% of children in lone parent families live in poverty;

- 34% of children living in families where someone has a disability are living in poverty;
- more than one third of children (36%) are living in families who are in deep poverty;
- 47% of children in Asian and British Asian families are living in poverty;
- 51% of children in Black/African/Caribbean and Black British families live in poverty.

These statistics raise a number of questions for wider policy and practice:

- What more can be done to cater for these 'hidden' children and young people?
- How can we focus attention on 'belonging' and 'inclusion for all' more widely?
- What more can be done to make sure that all schools have the opportunities, incentives and resources that they need to ensure inclusion for all?

Case Study: Temple Sutton Primary School and Nursery

Ola Laniyan - Head Teacher

At Temple Sutton Primary School, inclusion and equity underpin everything we do. We believe that every child deserves the opportunity to thrive - academically, socially and emotionally - regardless of background or starting point. Our approach focuses on removing barriers to learning through early identification, targeted interventions, and a culture of high expectations for all.

We recognise that disadvantage can take many forms - economic, social, linguistic or emotional - and that each child's experience is unique.

Our inclusion team works closely with teachers to identify needs early, whether through academic assessment, pastoral observations or parental conversations. Once identified, support is put in place swiftly and flexibly. This may include structured interventions in reading, writing or maths, additional tuition to close learning gaps or tailored mentoring to support confidence and wellbeing.

Strong pastoral care is central to our work. We operate a whole-school approach to emotional literacy and behaviour support, with nurture-based provision for pupils who need a more therapeutic approach. Our pastoral team liaises daily with families, external agencies and health professionals to ensure that each child's needs are met holistically. This wraparound care not only supports the child but strengthens family engagement and stability.

We understand that many barriers to learning exist beyond the classroom. To address this, we work with local partners to provide practical support to families - helping to access food banks, uniform assistance and signposting to housing and mental health services. This partnership approach ensures that no child's education is compromised by unmet basic needs.

Academic success is important, but so too is exposure to enriching experiences that broaden horizons and build cultural capital. Many of our pupils have limited opportunities to experience life beyond their immediate community, so we intentionally plan experiences - museum visits, theatre trips, residentials and community projects - that allow children to see themselves as part of a wider world. We also bring the world into school through visiting authors, artists and professionals who help pupils connect learning to future possibilities.

Case study question: How effectively do our current systems ensure that barriers to learning are identified early and addressed in ways that truly reflect each child's unique context and lived experience?

Potential Barriers That May Need to Be Reviewed

Funding and policies

- Since 2015, funding for inclusive education has been consistently reduced, suggesting that policymakers do not fully value equal access for all pupils. Schools are effectively having to deliver more for less.

Discrimination

- It's essential that schools work with their communities to reduce barriers for children with SEND, with EAL or from disadvantaged backgrounds to ensure that everyone is treated equally and nobody is ostracised by another group - it's important to refer to unconscious bias (discussed in the previous chapter) when thinking about how this may be addressed. Negative attitudes towards these groups of people can lead to them being overshadowed in classrooms and left out by peers.

Accessibility

- If a child cannot access their classroom, they are automatically excluded from the education they might receive. This could be due to the physical space, the ability to get to school for older children the language barriers or the perceptions of peers.

Lack of training

- Teaching pupils of varying abilities, who all learn in a different way, and some of whom have access needs, requires training. It's really important that teacher training providers cater for this within their syllabus and framework and include inclusion as part of the training.

Case Study: The Bishops' C of E and RC Primary School

Greg Waters – Head Teacher

There's never any obvious indication from us that a child or family is disadvantaged. Internally, their progress is monitored carefully – but so is their involvement.

It's made clear to everyone that every activity is there for every child. Clubs, trips, individual music lessons, residentials. We will financially support all of these, and we deliberately keep club places available for disadvantaged pupils in every club and quietly chase those (disadvantaged families) where their children are not doing any club. We prioritise opportunity over assessment, or monitoring, or core subjects – so if there's a chance to take the children to an event, a concert, or outside in the snow or leaves or wind – we do. Trips and/or visitors every term for every class.

We tutor pupils outside normal school hours (with our pupil premium [PP] funding). These are any pupils who need extra support but aren't already receiving interventions – and we prioritise the disadvantaged – 14 hour-long sessions in groups of three or four, led by Learning Support Assistants (LSAs) who have received training – and our data says that these tutored pupils' chances of making 'greater than expected progress' are well over those of pupils not receiving this support.

Being visionary for the vulnerable includes infusing the school experience with hope – every child is loved, every child is gifted, every child has a purpose, every child deserves our trust . . . in the life of each class, the themes for our assemblies/worship and we prioritise the wider curriculum – so that the full national curriculum entitlement for every pupil is given, and then we add to it with specialist music teaching, specialist sports coaching, specialist performing arts with public speaking.

A Reading Club (free) each morning before school tries to capture and support those pupils who, in Year 3 or above, are struggling readers. Many of these will be disadvantaged as their parents struggle to support them with schoolwork. Children who attend regularly make a year's progress in six months.

They celebrate effort, character, kindness, progress etc. every bit as much as attainment and academic success . . . through a simple award system where a child is identified in each class each week and given a 'Headteacher's Award' during the Friday assembly.

Other steps they take:

- *Vulnerable pupils who need it are welcomed individually at the school gates each morning by a regular member of staff.*

- *Every child is given a new, high-quality, children's book when they first come to school. This is to keep – so that there are no children without a book at home . . .*
- *Bedtime Story events for different year groups (FS to Year 2) get the children to school in their pyjamas in the evening for a story, some hot (warm) cocoa and a song . . . every child included if they possibly can . . .*
- *Early FS interventions such as whole-class Neli and Squiggle Wiggle support the early vocabulary and physical development of every child – and for those that are assessed through the screening as needing it, there are almost daily individual/small group sessions of Neli. Catching them early and developing their skills as early as possible is seen as a vital investment in their future learning . . .*
- *Play, play, play in FS and in school life develops the capacity of all pupils to experience the positivity of social, fun, community experiences . . . and this develops their confidence and their hope . . .*
- *School uniform has been simplified so that it is less expensive, and there is second-hand clothing always available in school . . .*
- *Carers Club for pupils who identify themselves as any kind of carer in their family, for example as carers of parents or siblings with special needs etc . . .*
- *Every child receives a Bible – a very special book for school and then home . . .*
- *We monitor and support attendance carefully and sensitively. We never fine.*
- *Pastoral support (for children and their families) and counselling always available.*
- *Christmas presents and food parcels for vulnerable families, supported by local charities . . .*
- *Luna, our school dog, and chickens – animals which create an extra dimension of belonging for all . . .*
- *Breakfast box in staffroom for children who need it . . .*
- *Governors' monitoring of PP children is regular, both their progress and attainment but also their attitudes, sense of support and involvement in the wider life of the school.*
- *Free places at breakfast club and after school club when vulnerable pupils/families* need them.
- *'Keep children in mind' – our practice of ensuring that our vulnerable pupils are thought about when we are not with them . . .'I was thinking about you yesterday . . .' ('Every interaction is an intervention').*
- *We have the progress of disadvantaged pupils and their provision regularly discussed through our performance management progress.*
- *Try to live up to our motto . . . and ensure that every member of our community can say we . . .*

'Live Fully, Laugh Often, Learn Deeply, Love as God Loves You, . . .

and Let Your Light Shine!'

Case study question: How does your school vision, motto or ethos live out through your school community?

Practical Ideas to Support with Inclusion

Gaining a holistic view of the students

- Capture a holistic profile on each student. Teachers should have a conversation with each child, as part of their transition into a new class/school about their interests. Find out what motivates them. This helps teachers tailor their teaching to match each child's needs and helps when writing any kind of modifications and assessments to use in their weekly lesson plan.
- Within this profile, there should be information about gender, age, language. This should be done in collaboration with parents and carers.
- There could be opportunities for information sharing with previous schools. For example, how do the students learn? What are their learning habits like? Is there information about any specialists' observations if they have SEN or a disability?
- Teachers must talk to specialists and study students' previous assessments, inside and outside the classroom.
- Getting to know the children should include observations.

Other areas which need attention when addressing inclusion:

Attendance

Disadvantaged pupils are more likely to be absent from school. The Education Policy Institute reveals that if disadvantaged students had the same level of attendance as their peers, the GCSE gap would be four months smaller. They go on to say that the impact of absence has grown over time with the widest gap between 2019 to 2023 (EPI, 2025). Although the whole picture of absence needs to be examined, there is clearly a link between persistent absence and disengagement.

Absence can signal a few things, but it must be remembered that it is always context dependent. This is important to note because what works well for one student in a particular context won't always work for another. Research conducted by Impact Ed showed that when students feel a sense of belonging and feel part of a community then there is a correlation with high attendance and motivation (Goodenow, 1993, cited in ImpactEd, 2024). Furthermore, pupils with the highest attendance rate had a high 'sense of school membership'. As outlined by Sims (2024, p. 26) 'pupils' sense of belonging is hampered by their attendance rates and vice versa'.

Positive signs of belonging in schools:

- Attending awards ceremonies
- Wanting to wear school uniform
- Good relationships with teachers
- A circle of friends.

Allen and Kern (2017)

Negative impact on belonging:

- Poor attendance
- exclusion
- Peer influence

Allen and Kern (2017)

The data also revealed, not surprisingly, that this is especially the case for pupils in receipt of the pupil premium 'whose sense of belonging scores are three per cent below their non pupil premium peers'. We know that children from disadvantaged communities are twice as likely as their more advantaged peers to feel that they don't belong (Riley, Coalter and White, 2020). The relationships that children and young people have with adults in school is one of the most important factors to addressing this. Their sense of belonging is cultivated and maintained through these relationships and should not be underestimated. Another crucial factor is a student's level of engagement and participating in school activities. Pupils with high engagement show stronger resilience 'and are less likely to drop out of school' (Wang and Fredericks, 2014).

- Student-teacher relationships – the most significant factor for pupils' sense of belonging is their relationship with their teacher.
- Student voice – encourage pupil involvement.

Research suggests that parental/family engagement is more influential on pupil attainment than many school-based interventions. For example, Henderson and Berla concluded from 66 studies that the *most accurate predictor* of student achievement is the level of family involvement (Henderson and Berla, 1994).

Similarly, Henderson and Mapp (2002) argue that sustained partnerships between schools and families are central to improving student outcomes.

Parental Engagement

Indeed, the value of parental engagement in schools cannot be underestimated (Bond, Moore and Hawkins, 2025). Parental engagement has the greatest impact on pupil attainment than any other aspect of schooling. It is widely recognised as a crucial factor in supporting children's educational success, yet its significance becomes even more pronounced for disadvantaged pupils (Lasater, Crowe and Pijanowski, 2023). Children from socio-economically challenged backgrounds often face additional barriers to learning – including limited access to resources, reduced confidence and less familiarity with navigating the school system. In this context, strong home-school partnerships are not simply an 'added extra'; they are a vital lever for equity.

The Education Endowment Foundation in their 'Parental Engagement Toolkit' (2025a) suggest the following for implementing a successful strategy:

- Tailor communication to encourage positive dialogue about learning.
- Regularly reviewing how well the school is working with parents and identifying areas for improvement.
- Offer more sustained and intrinsic support where needed.

When a child's family is involved in their education, children perform better academically, their attendance is better and they are secure both emotionally and socially. A study carried out by (Bond, Moore and Hawkins, 2025) revealed that some schools provided opportunities for engagement with families, but that any blame for lack of involvement or engagement centred very much on the parents. The study concluded that ideally, there needs to be a societal understanding of the impact of poverty and hardship on all aspects of a family's life including their ability to participate in their child's school and learning (Bond, Moore and Hawkins, 2025, p. 17).

What can be taken from this? Educators must adopt a flexible approach to communicating with parents. Communication must be clear and focused on building rapport and trust. Any potential barriers must be considered.

How to build strong links with families:

- Think about how you communicate with families.
- Send the same message out to families via an email, through an app, printed letter or social media.
- If families need more specialised communications due to language barriers, SEND requirements or accessibility needs, schools can create groups in the system to ensure they only receive communications that are relevant to their needs.

Curriculum

A high-quality education which is designed to meet the needs of children and provide an inclusive education is the foundation for social improvement (Eden, 2024). Inclusion is an ongoing process focused on continually improving learning and participation for every student. To develop this point further, an inclusive curriculum should support everyone – from students, teachers and parents as well as other stakeholders (LI, 2022). An inclusive curriculum has the capacity to empower students to have agency over their own learning journey. Therefore, it can be said that a school's curricula is an investment in our young people's future.

In the pursuit of inclusive curriculum design, it is imperative for educators to deeply understand and address the diverse needs of students (Akintayo et al., 2024).

When we consider the term curriculum, one might think that this is the content or syllabus that is covered in the range of subjects being taught, which of course it is - but we can think of this as curricula - essentially everything that is covered in school. From the content of assemblies to trips which are scheduled for the academic year. We can also refer to this as a 'local curriculum' (Hill and Kershaw, 2025). This allows schools to develop a curriculum that fits the context of the school. By doing this, schools can create more meaningful learning opportunities that specifically address the needs of the most disadvantaged pupils. Schools may well state that their curriculum is underpinned by certain principles. For example, wanting children and young people to become successful learners. But, if the school experience, learning environments and extra-curricular activities fail to reflect these ideals, these efforts become tokenistic.

Certainly, young people will engage in their learning more deeply when the information is relatable, and meaningful - or when they can make connections with real-life experiences (Murray, 2022).

> While learners often make natural connections in exploratory settings, structured academic environments can separate knowledge into rigid subject areas, making it essential to adopt holistic teaching practices that support the transfer of learning across different contexts, to develop mind, curiosity and persistence.
>
> (Hill and Kershaw, 2025, p. 4)

Teachers and educators can ensure that the curriculum is inclusive by employing strategic pedagogical approaches. These approaches are deliberate methods used to design, sequence and deliver learning so that all pupils make progress. Strategic pedagogy ensures that learning is purposeful, inclusive and rooted in a deep understanding of how children learn. By designing learning experiences that enable young people to develop critical thinking, student agency, educators can empower learners with lifelong skills. Skills such as questioning bias, empathy, appreciating different viewpoints and taking an active role in their own education. Skills which are not just needed in school, but essential in life.

Key strategies for this inclusive curriculum design:

- Set clear learning objectives;
- Use a range of teaching methods;
- Use adaptive teaching methods - adapting to the needs of the pupils in the moment;
- Foster collaboration;
- Use technology;
- Regularly review the curriculum offer;
- Create a stimulating learning environment;
- Experiential learning.

The Experiential Learning model above demonstrates the continual cycle of learning by 'doing' which is then followed by 'reflection'. Essentially, students learn from their

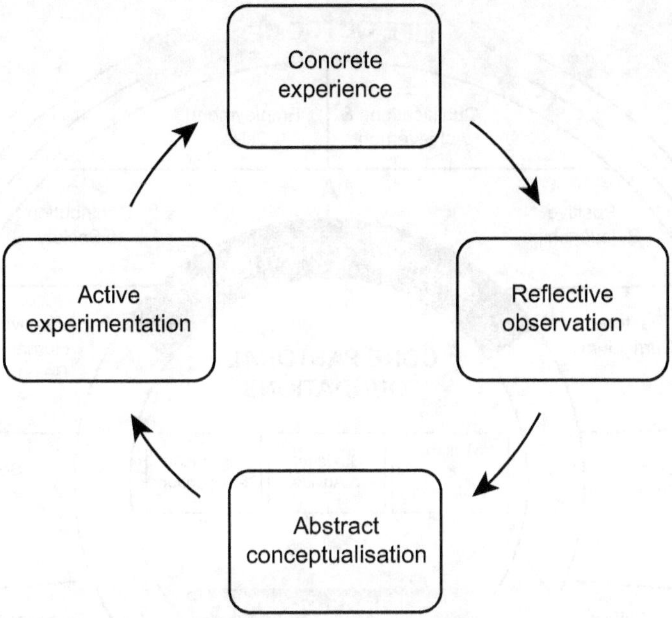

Figure 4.2 Kolb's Experiential learning cycle

(Adapted from Kolb, 1984)

experiences and so teachers consider the quality of these experiences, as each new experience builds upon previous learning and experiences.

Other Curriculum Considerations

Teacher autonomy over curriculum content and pedagogical approach is shaped and often constrained by wider policy decisions. Much of what teachers are required to teach is determined by policymakers operating at national or systemic levels, which means classroom practice is influenced by decisions made far beyond the school itself. However, knowing your students is essential. Ask yourself what these particular students in this community need to lead fulfilled lives. The image below demonstrates how all the various aspects of school life fit together similar to a jigsaw puzzle.

How Else Can Schools Build a Culture of Inclusion?

We all want an education system where all young people can thrive, but for some children the school day can become expensive and essentially, they can be priced out. The Child Poverty Action Group (CPAG) research (2025) shows clearly that not being able to afford school uniform or pay for a school trip, afford the school supplies and pay for transport to school are key reasons why children are missing school. We know that the odd missed day can easily turn into persistent absence.

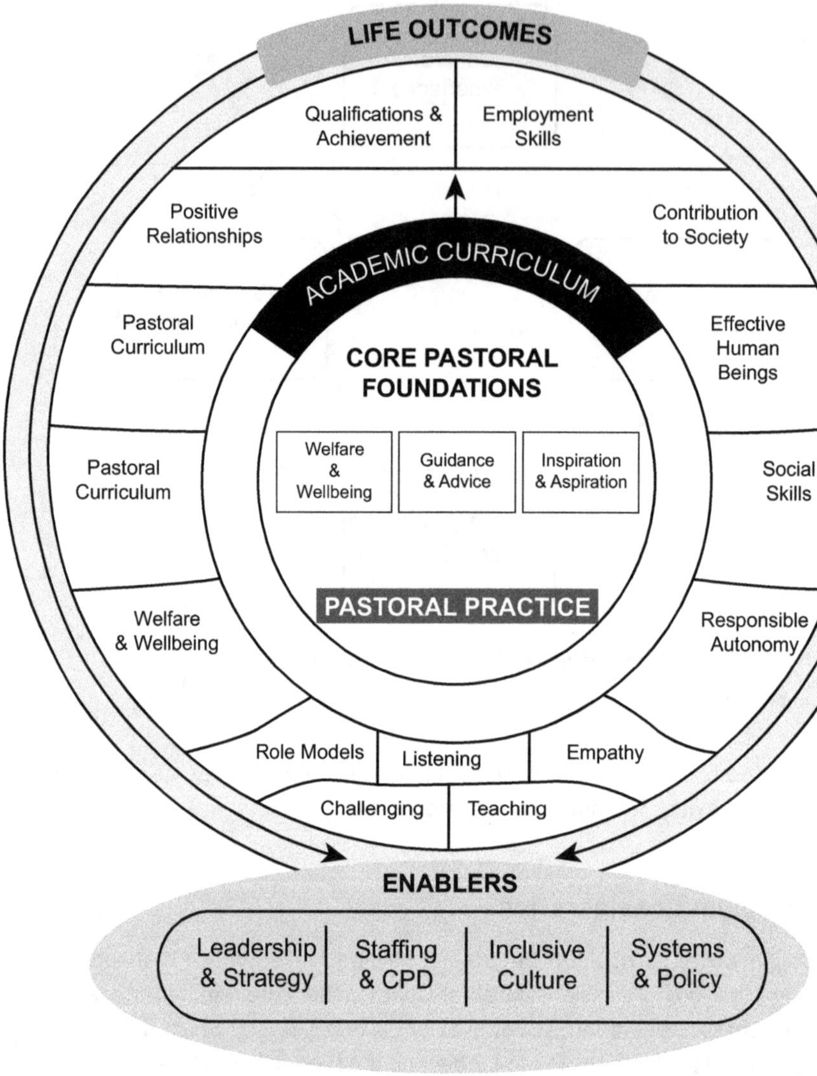

Figure 4.3 The Pastoral impact framework

(Adapted from Marland, 1974; Noddings, 2005; Carpenter, 2015)

Case Study: Becket Keys Secondary School, Brentwood, Essex

Andy Scott-Evans, Head Teacher

At our school, inclusion is not an additional policy or programme; it is central to our vision of enabling every student to 'bear fruit that will last' (John 15:16). We see each child as uniquely gifted by God and seek to nurture their academic, emotional and spiritual growth in a community where all belong and are valued.

Our approach to inclusion is both strategic and relational. Strategically, we ensure that barriers to learning are identified early and addressed through high-quality teaching, carefully planned routines and a well-structured curriculum. Relationally, we cultivate a culture of compassion, respect and high expectation, where difference is seen as a source of strength and richness.

Our most recent Ofsted report (February 2025) described our approach to inclusion as 'exemplary', noting that pupils with special educational needs and/or disabilities 'access the full curriculum alongside their peers and achieve exceptionally well'. Inspectors also highlighted the way sixth-form students mentor younger pupils, helping them to develop a love of reading; something we see as a lived expression of our Christian commitment to service and fellowship.

Inclusion at our school is also about participation. We make sure that every student has access to the full life of the school, most importantly in the curriculum itself, but also in other ways such as leadership roles, enrichment activities, worship, and service opportunities. We aim to create an environment where every young person, whatever their starting point or need, can thrive and know that they are deeply valued.

Case study question: How consistently do our everyday teaching practices and relationships reflect our belief that every child is uniquely gifted and called to flourish within our school community?

Research into the cost of school uniforms reveals that families spend almost £450 for basic secondary school uniform, bags and PE kit (Child Poverty Action Group, 2025). Education has become significantly more expensive since 2022, with costs rising by 16% for primary children and a striking 30% for secondary students, far outpacing inflation and wage growth. Families are feeling the strain, driven by rising food costs, the growing need for digital devices and higher subject costs like art and design materials.

How can we embed poverty sensitive school practices so that children are not priced out of the school day?

- Limit the number of branded uniform items to no more than three.
- Provide all learning materials.
- Provide a large, zipped wallet rather than a branded book bag.
- Actively advertise second-hand uniform.
- Rather than dressing up for World Book Days, decorate the classroom door or display board.
- Limit the number of fundraising events to no more than 1 or 2 per term.

- Restrict or do away with non-uniform days.
- Ensure that school fairs always have a free element to them.
- Provide technology for children to complete homework before and after school or during a lunch time.
- Where a school trip needs payment, ensure this is given well in advance.
- Actively keep open communication and support available for families regarding financial matters.
- Look at fundraising opportunities beyond the school.
- Don't assume that all families in an affluent area are financially well off.

Chapter Takeaways

Reflections

- Inclusion is intentional and relational: A culture of inclusion does not happen by chance; it is purposefully designed through strong relationships, equity-driven practice and a whole-school commitment where every pupil, staff member and family feels a genuine sense of belonging.
- Knowing the whole child is essential: Effective inclusion depends on deeply understanding pupils' lives, backgrounds, barriers and strengths beyond surface data such as attainment or free school meal status, recognising that disadvantage is complex and often hidden.
- Poverty and inequality are multidimensional: Disadvantage is not limited to unemployment and affects many working families, larger families, lone-parent households, disabled families and some ethnic groups disproportionately.
- Belonging drives outcomes: Research consistently shows that strong student-teacher relationships, pupil voice, participation in school life and family engagement are central to improving attendance, wellbeing, resilience and academic success, particularly for disadvantaged pupils.
- Inclusive practice must be systemic and practical: Successful inclusion requires evidence-informed strategies across curriculum design, pedagogy, pastoral care, family partnerships and poverty-sensitive policies.

Now Consider

- In what ways is inclusion actively designed in your school, rather than assumed?
- Which pupils might be 'invisible' within our systems, and why?
- How confident are we in identifying barriers that pupils themselves may not articulate?
- How do we ensure staff understanding of poverty moves beyond assumptions or stereotypes?
- How do relationships, engagement and participation feature in our measures of success?
- What would 'poverty-proofing' the school day look like in practice for your setting?

Enhanced Provision and Ideas to Support Learning

- Consider the cost of uniform.
- How do you ensure strong communications with your families?
- In what ways is inclusion actively designed in your school, rather than assumed?
- Which pupils might be 'invisible' within our systems, and why?
- How confident are we in identifying barriers that pupils themselves may not articulate?
- How do we ensure staff understanding of poverty moves beyond assumptions or stereotypes?
- How do relationships, engagement and participation feature in our measures of success?
- What would 'poverty-proofing' the school day look like in practice for your setting?

Further Reading

- Education Endowment Foundation (2025). *Implementing the Pupil Premium Strategy.* London. Education Endowment Foundation.
- Rowland, S. (2021; 2025). *Rethinking pupil premium and inclusive practice.* Woodbridge: John Catt Educational.
- Akintayo, O.T., Eden, C.A., Ayeni, O.O. and Onyebuchi, N.C. (2024) 'Inclusive curriculum design: Meeting the diverse needs of students for social improvement'. *International Journal of Frontiers in Science and Technology Research*, 6(2), 50–59. https://doi.org/10.53294/ijfstr.2024.6.2.0037.
- Sean Harris and Katrina Morley (2025) *Tackling Poverty and Disadvantage in Schools.* London: Bloomsbury Education.

Bibliography

Adobe Stock. (2024). *Students collaborating in a classroom* [Photograph]. https://stock.adobe.com.

Akintayo, O.T., Eden, C.A., Ayeni, O.O. and Onyebuchi, N.C. (2024). 'Inclusive curriculum design: Meeting the diverse needs of students for social improvement'. *International Journal of Frontiers in Science and Technology Research*, 6(2), 50–59. https://doi.org/10.53294/ijfstr.2024.6.2.0037.

Allen, K.A. and Kern, M.L. (2017). *School belonging in adolescents: Theory, research and practice.* Singapore: Springer.

Bond, A., Moore, G. and Hawkins, J. (2025) 'Understanding parental involvement with schools and parental engagement with learning across schools in areas of socioeconomic deprivation in Wales'. *Educational Review.* https://www.tandfonline.com/doi/full/10.1080/00131911.2024.2432255.

British Council. (July 2025). 'Leading inclusion and belonging in schools'. *British Council.*

Cameron, C. (2025). *Urban childhoods: Growing up in inequality and hope.* London: UCL Press. https://discovery.ucl.ac.uk/id/eprint/10212736/1/Urban-Childhoods.pdf.

Carpenter, B. (2015). *A recovery curriculum: Loss and life for our children and schools post pandemic.* London: Evidence for Learning.

Child Poverty Action Group. (May 2025). 'The minimum cost of education in the UK'. cpag.org.uk.

Child Poverty Action Group. (29 May 2025). 'Priced out of school – how lack of money prevents young people from attending school'. *Child Poverty in the UK*. https://cpag.org.uk/child-poverty.
Child Poverty Action Group. (2025). 'What is poverty?' https://cpag.org.uk/child-poverty/what-poverty.
The Children's Society. (2023). 'The Good Childhood Report 2023'. https://www.childrenssociety.org.uk/information/professionals/resources/good-childhood-report-2023.
Eden, C. (2024). 'Inclusive curriculum design: Meeting the diverse needs of students for social improvement'. *International Journal of Frontiers in Science and Technology Research*. https://www.researchgate.net/profile/Nneamaka-Onyebuchi-4/publication/390162935_Inclusive_curriculum_design_Meeting_the_diverse_needs_of_students_for_social_improvement/links/67e78c889b1c6c487761f296/Inclusive-curriculum-design-Meeting-the-diverse-needs-of.
Education Endowment Foundation. (2025a). *Teaching and Learning Toolkit: Parental Engagement*. London: Education Endowment Foundation. https://educationendowmentfoundation.org.uk/education-evidence/teaching-learning-toolkit/parental-engagement.
Education Endowment Foundation. (2025b). 'The EEF Guide to the Pupil Premium'. https://educationendowmentfoundation.org.uk/using-pupil-premium/diagnose-your-pupils-needs.
Education Policy Institute (EPI) (2025). *Annual Report 2025: Access and outcomes for disadvantaged pupils*. London: Education Policy Institute.
Greany, T., Pennacchia, J., Graham, J. and Bernardes, E. (2024) *Belonging schools: How do relatively more inclusive secondary schools approach and practise inclusion?* London: Teach First. https://www.teachfirst.org.uk/reports/belonging-schools.
Henderson, A.T. and Berla, N. (eds.) (1994). *A new generation of evidence: The family is critical to student achievement*. Washington, DC: National Committee for Citizens in Education.
Henderson, A.T. and Mapp, K.L. (2002). *A new wave of evidence: The impact of school, family, and community connections on student achievement*. Austin, TX: Southwest Educational Development Laboratory (SEDL).
Hill, S. and Kershaw, D. (2025). 'Towards a holistic education: Inclusive curriculum design for student growth'. *Impact*, 24.
ImpactEd. (2024). *Belonging: The importance of connection, community and inclusion in schools*. London: ImpactEd Group.
Kolb, D.A. (1984). *Experiential learning: Experience as the source of learning and development*. Englewood Cliffs, NJ: Prentice-Hall.
Lasater, K., Crowe, T.C. and Pijanowski, J. (2023). 'Developing family-school partnerships in the midst of demographic change: An examination of educators' attitudes, values, and beliefs and the discourses they shape'. *Leadership and Policy in Schools*, *22*(2), 347–368. https://doi.org/10.1080/15700763.2021.195886.
Li, E. (2022). 'Developing and inclusive curriculum: What can we learn from teachers' inclusive pedagogy?' *Impact*, 14, 74–75.
Marland, M. (1974). *Pastoral care*. London: Heinemann.
Murray, J. (2022) 'Young children's curriculum: Principles, practice and issues'. *International Journal of Early Years Education*, 30(4).
Noddings, N. (2005). *The challenge to care in schools: An alternative approach to education*. 2nd edn. New York: Teachers College Press.
Oracy Education Commission. (2024). *We need to talk*. https://oracyeducationcommission.co.uk/wp-content/uploads/2024/10/Future-of-Oracy-v23-web-13.pdf.
Riley, K., Coalter, J. and White, H. (2020) *Place and belonging in schools: Why it matters today*. London: UCL Institute of Education.
Rowland, M. (2021). *Addressing educational disadvantage in schools and colleges: The Essex way*. Woodbridge: John Catt Educational.
Sims, C. (2024). 'The drivers behind attendance: What we are learning about the importance of belonging, engagement, sanctions and support'. *Impact*, 20, 25–27.
Strand, S. (2021). *The educational achievement of white British pupils: New evidence on the role of poverty and ethnicity*. London: Educational Policy Institute.
Wang, M.-T. and Fredricks, J.A. (2014) 'The reciprocal links between school engagement, youth problem behaviors, and school dropout during adolescence'. *Child Development*, 85(2), 722–737.

5 Why Diversity in the Curriculum Matters

Diversity in the curriculum matters because it directly shapes how children see themselves, others and the world. A diverse curriculum is not an 'add-on', it is a foundation for equity, belonging and high expectations – particularly in a more diverse world. A diverse curriculum intentionally disrupts narrow or harmful narratives, encourages empathy and challenges rigid viewpoints. It broadens what is considered 'normal' and challenges assumptions, helping pupils recognise and question bias in society.

Pre-reading Reflection Questions

- To what extent does your curriculum/subject enable all pupils and young people to feel seen and represented rather than tokenistically?
- How might the texts, books, resources, scheme of work that you use reinforce, ignore or challenge power imbalances?
- In what ways does your school/curricula provide time to actively encourage young people to question assumptions, debate different points of view, recognise bias and engage with different cultures?
- How well do your teaching approaches respond equitably to all young people. How do your interventions address this?
- What systems are in place to evaluate your efforts to diversity and decolonise the curriculum.
- How do you measure the impact?

Diverse Communities

We live in an increasingly diverse world. Our school communities witness this. Over the last 20 years, schools have become more diverse. In June 2025, the Department for Education published a report highlighting that the percentage of children whose first language is not English is increasing year on year across England (GOV.UK, 2025). In the academic year

DOI: 10.4324/9781003624004-5

2024/25, approximately 21.4% of pupils at schools in England did not speak English as their first language; this is compared to approximately 18% of pupils in the academic year 2015/16. These figures show that the share of pupils whose first language is not English has risen steadily in recent years, which reflects the broader demographic changes in the school population across England. This rise in children with a first language which is not English, impacts the diversity of a school community and this diversity must be recognised and represented. Figure 5.1 below illustrates this trend:

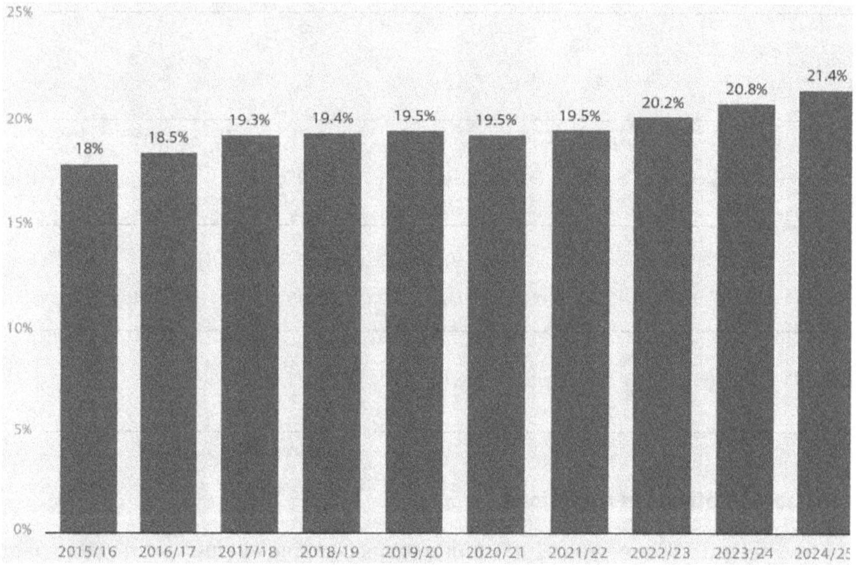

Figure 5.1 Persistent absence rates in England, 2015/16-2024/25

(Department for Education, 2025)

A report by The Bell Foundation explored this data further, also recognising that there is a huge regional variation in the number of EAL children, and thus the number of cultures within schools depending on the area. The schools with the highest percentage of EAL children are found in the most urban areas of the country - most notably London, the West Midlands and the North West. In these areas the numbers are significantly higher than other parts of the county - in London nearly half (47.9%) of all schools have over 50% of their school community registered as EAL, this is 13.2% in the West Midlands and 11.6% in the North West. However, this is an unreliable measure of ethnic status, as many schools report significantly higher actual figures. We must prepare to face an increasingly diverse world and therefore in our schools. The UK's population is expected to continue to diversify ethnically in the forthcoming years (Lomax et al., 2019).

How Diverse Are Our Schools?

In response to our increasingly diverse schools and settings, educators must try to ensure their school curricula is representative of the students in their school. McKeating (2022) notes that 'Representation is important for all children to see themselves in learning... and have role models in the school' (p. 342). Crucially, the point is emphasised that 'when we cannot see ourselves in the world around us this creates limited beliefs, a fixed mindset on what is achievable and increases othering' (McKeating, cited in *Impact*, 2025). Essentially, what is being taught in schools needs to be helpful to all students and representative of the diverse students in the school.

Biesta (2021) asserts that education is about helping prepare students for the world. Rather than imparting skills and knowledge, he talks about 'an act of (re)directing the attention of students to the world'. Essentially, school must be viewed as the place 'where the new generation is given the time to meet the world and meet themselves in relation to the world' (Biesta, 2021).

In 2020, Pearson conducted a survey of school staff to explore perceptions of diversity within education. Notably, 80% of respondents indicated that greater efforts were needed to better support diverse cultures, identities and lived experiences (Pearson, 2020). However, fostering diversity extends beyond promoting a sense of belonging within the school community. A diverse curriculum enables students to engage with the full breadth of human experience, allowing them to encounter narratives and representations that reflect their own identities while also developing empathy and understanding for those whose experiences differ from their own (Brett and Brassington, 2023, p. 52).

What Is a Definition of Diversity?

The earliest definition of the term diversity was in 1150-1500 (Oxford English Dictionary) where the term was referred to as a quality or condition. More recently, the Collins dictionary (2025) defines the terms as 'Something that contains many very different elements'. Diversity gained prominence in the mid-20th century as a social and cultural term. Today, diversity encompasses a broad range of identities with the expansion of the term 'diversity' reflecting the broader understanding of what it symbolises.

In terms of education, the most recent UK National Curriculum and Assessment Review (CAR) emphasises integrating and embedding diversity more. The interim report (Department for Education, 2025) recommends greater representation of ethnicities and other diversities. The report also puts forward that the National Curriculum should have more focus on social diversity and more emphasis upon citizenship (Department for Education, 2025).

Broader Benefits of a Diverse Curriculum

Being diverse ensures that pupils of all ages are engaged in and encouraged to consider a range of viewpoints and opinions. It encourages critical thinking skills which are important beyond the gates of the school, as well as developing empathy and helping to prepare children for the diverse, multicultural world in which they live. By reducing bias, stereotypes and giving all children and young people accurate and inclusive representations of the world in which they are citizens, schools go some way to provide a curriculum which 'is a window into the world' (Kara, 2024, p. 3).

What are the ultimate goals of an education and a curriculum? We know that there is so much more than exam results. It is also about teaching young people about being human. What policy makers decide is important to teach in the National Curriculum, is what we are saying is the most important knowledge young people need to know to live successful and happy lives. Through the curriculum, schools can teach their students about injustice and morality. Kara (2024) explains further, she tells us that 'it is about seeing outside of oneself . . . exposing students to a wider range of opinions improves the quality of those students' intellectual advancement' (Kara, 2024, p. 4).

Kara (2024) has developed a table with an overview of the role of schools in diversifying the curriculum:

Table 5.1 The diverse curriculum

Institutional Stance	*Underlying Belief*	*Curriculum Expression*
Maintenance	No change is needed	Status quo remains dominant
Reinforcement	Some groups are less legitimate	Curriculum actively marginalises certain communities
Transformation	Curriculum shapes justice	Diverse knowledge systems are embedded and foregrounded

(Adapted from Kara, 2024)

While schools do not intentionally set out to reinforce prejudice, they might well ignore prejudice because they have not carefully considered the knowledge they are teaching.

Developing a diverse and inclusive curriculum should begin at home – ensuring that all ethnic groups are recognised and represented. It should then be built from the school around the local community, the county, country and wider world. For children, it allows them to celebrate their own cultures, their own ethnicity, disabilities and individual differences. Diversity within education can also help to combat misconceptions and unconscious bias that may have been instilled from an early age, and makes pupils feel more welcome and included in the school community. It helps to positively shape interactions with others, and to understand the roots of certain issues. It is important for them to respect everyone and treat each other equally. If a curriculum is culturally and socially diverse it is a powerful tool for helping to address social justice and historical injustice. It opens pupils' eyes to enabling them to see different perspectives and highlights the complexities of an ever-changing world. Literature, which we will come on to later in this chapter, is a powerful tool for enabling this. Aside from individual representation there is evidence that having a diverse curriculum engages and motivates learners of all ages.

Case Study: The Bishops School, Chelmsford, Essex

Liz Lee, EYFS Lead

While teaching phonics recently at The Bishops School in Chelmsford, Liz Lee (EYFS Lead) shared that a Foundation Stage child shouted out during the session: 'That boy is like me?' Another child said, 'No he isn't, he has blonde hair!' The first child responded and pointed out, 'Look that boy has a hearing aid and so do I – we are the same!' In future lessons multiple children talked about the boy in the slides and pointed out that it looked like their friend – they asked questions about the hearing aid and this led to conversations about its importance and purpose – representation is essential for children to feel included and equal.

Case study question: How does the representation we choose in our teaching materials shape children's sense of belonging, identity and understanding of difference?

The above case study highlights the importance of recognising differences and knowing that this is okay. This is where it is important to recognise the difference between equality and equity.

Equity: Understands that people are not the same and have individual needs.
Equality: Can assume that everyone is the same and should be treated this way.

Knowing this difference is important when considering how to create a diverse curriculum. As Kara (2024) believes 'equality is an end point; equity should be seen as the process by which we reach equality' (Kara, 2024, p. 14). This is what we aim to do in the classroom – we recognise the wide range of different starting points of children in the classroom – and they require more scaffolding and modelling. Whatever the needs of the child and how we adapt our teaching – this is thinking equitably.

What else needs to be considered?

Decolonisation

This is the consideration given to how the knowledge, which is taught in the National Curriculum, is chosen and where the knowledge comes from. It means challenging power relations and reflecting upon the content and how this is delivered. For example, a review of curriculum content often reveals a substantial disparity in the representation of men and women.

The impact of this in our classrooms is that if teachers, leaders and policy makers do not consider certain biases (such as the gender bias highlighted above) then what message is this giving to our students? This can of course be applied to all subjects. If the scientists children meet first are all male and white, what message does this communicate to young people? We must think about the visibility we are giving to different people.

Table 5.2 Named figures in the National Curriculum by gender

Men	*Women*
John Dunlop	Jane Goodall
Charles Mackintosh	Ruth Benerito
John McAdam	Mary Anning
David Attenborough	Elizabeth I
Spencer Silver	Rosa Parks
Galileo Galilei	Emily Davidson
Isaac Newton	Mary Seacole
Carl Linnaeus	Florence Nightingale
Charles Darwin	Edith Cavell
Alfred Wallace	Rosaline Franklin
Christopher Columbus	
Neil Armstrong	
William Caxton	
Tim Berners-Lee	
Pieter Bruegel the Elder	
L.S. Lowry	
William Shakespeare	
Pythagoras	
Watson, Crick and Wilkins	
Johan Dalton	
Robert Hookr	
Henry VII	
Cromwell	

(Kara, 2024, p. 44)

The University of Liverpool uses the Figure 5.2 infographic as a structure in assessing the diversity of a curriculum. They highlight the following need to be evaluated. For example, what is the demographic profile of authors being used in class? To what extent do programmes/subjects/modules enable the use of non-English sources in the curriculum?

In response to this, think about these questions:

- How can curricula meaningfully include the voices, histories, art, cultures and lived experiences of people from a wide range of backgrounds?
- How can we ensure that representations of women extend beyond white women to include women from the global majority?
- Where are there opportunities to foreground and celebrate the achievements of individuals from the global majority?
- How can discussions of LGBTQ+ identities be inclusive of people from diverse religious, cultural and national contexts?

There are various ways in which schools can facilitate this change in curricula.

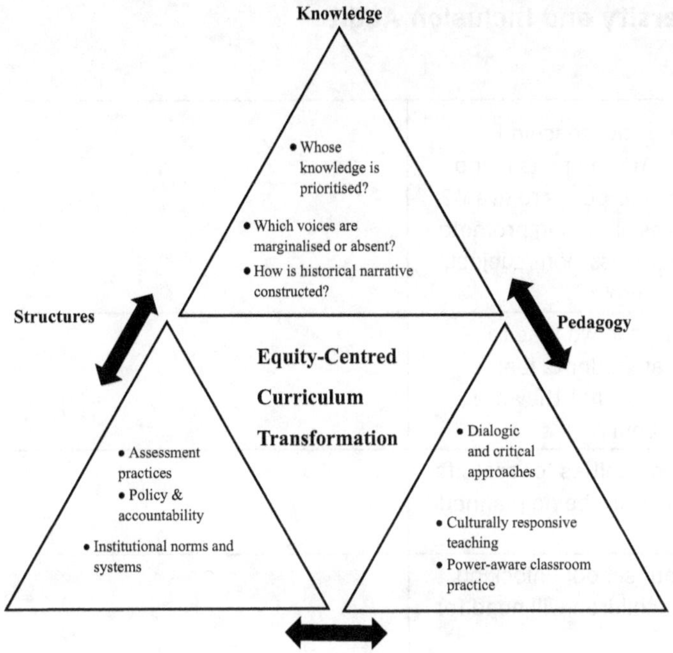

Figure 5.2 A framework for decolonising educational practice

(Adapted from Munoz, 2025, University of Liverpool)

Review these questions:

What are the barriers to learning that pupils are experiencing and in which subjects?	**What are their strengths, interests and aspirations?**
What support do they need to access the curriculum?	**How can the school's provision be improved to support these pupils to learn?**

School-wide – review the following:

- Provide dedicated time to update subject knowledge with clear steps and goals.
- Provide dedicated budget for specific subject knowledge development such as membership of the subject association, e.g. geography.
- Encourage staff to attend CPD on developing diverse knowledge and skills .

Within subject areas complete the following audit:

Diversity and Inclusion Audit

1. Reevaluate your teaching materials. Are the texts being taught to your pupils relevant? What voices are being promoted within your classroom/subject/school/setting?	
2. What steps can we take to ensure that students feel connected to what they are learning about?	
3. What opportunities for real-life experiences are being planned for?	
4. How is your school unlocking skills that children will need for the future?	
5. How are you organising seating plans?	
6. Do you pre-teach? How could this be organised?	
7. Give students agency - what would they like to see?	
8. Reach out to other schools in your area who have started/already diversified and decolonised their curriculum.	
9. Ensure you are creating a safe space for discussion.	
10. How are interventions completed? Organised?	

Completing the above provides the time to evaluate existing planning, learning materials and schemes of work. Look to see where diverse perspectives can be included in all subject areas. Think of ways in which you can collaborate with the local community too.

- It is worth working with the local community in making changes to the curriculum. This will ensure that the material is moderated and authentic.
- This also provides the opportunity to include the community thereby strengthening relationships and reducing potential conflicts.

Practical Approaches and Resources

In order to support the changes made, it is vital to ensure that school staff lead by example. The staff in the school are first and foremost role models. They must model inclusive behaviour. Regular audits of 'diversity' within the school should be undertaken. Select resources (books, music and historical figures that demonstrate diverse perspectives and experiences). Challenge students to look at problems from different viewpoints.

Classroom/school walls: what are the children and young people seeing everyday? What are the colour and gender of the toys the young children play with? Which role models are displayed on the school walls? Who said those quotes? What words and phrases are used to speak with the young people? What music are they listening to? Question whether the environment you are creating is providing a widow into the world? Is it representative of the wider world?

The case study below explores how a school made some steps to improve the humanities curriculum:

Case Study: Bishops C of E and RC Primary School

At a school in Chelmsford, 30 miles east of London, a post-pandemic review of the Humanities curriculum identified that their 'Earth Explorer' topic only had explorers who were from a white European background (and who were also dead!). After researching explorers and considering the school's demographic make-up, which had changed dramatically over the last decade, they decided to continue teaching about Earnest Shackleton but complement this with work on modern-day explorer Namira Salim. During the teaching of this unit of work, the children were particularly engaged and the girls were more eager to participate than in previous years. After teaching this unit of work, a parent approached the staff and thanked them. The parent said her daughter had been so excited to tell them at home about the learning and had told her parents that she didn't know she could be an explorer or an astronaut because she didn't see any Indian girls doing this. After learning about Namira, she wanted to explore the world and be just like her!

Case study question: How can including diverse role models in the curriculum influence students' aspirations and engagement, particularly for those from underrepresented groups?

Through ensuring that every child in the class or school community is represented in some way helps to boost children's self-esteem, their belief in themselves, and shows them that there are no limits to what they can be and who they can become. By celebrating and representing children in a classroom, it ensures that every pupil feels welcomed, acknowledged and seen.

Case Study: Why Diversity Matters Within Every Curriculum

Andrew Moffat, No Outsiders

Why is there a huge white sign hanging 500 metres from the front entrance of my school with the words, 'Raise the colours, Stop the boats, Realism not racism, Save our kids' scrawled across a St George's flag? Why are there smaller flags hanging from every lamp-post as you walk towards my school and how do they make the children in my school feel as they walk in the gates?

My school is diverse in many ways; nationalities, language, disability, religion . . . It's a microcosm of the UK today in the same way most schools are today. In Y6 on the first day back in the new academic year, we talked about who belongs in our school and set out our culture. In my school we use No Outsiders to teach children that everyone belongs; there are 'no outsiders' here because everyone is welcome. No Outsiders uses lesson plans based on picture books to explore difference and inclusion. There is an emphasis on oracy and pupils are taught to listen to different points of view while forming their own opinions. A No Outsiders lesson does not teach pupils what to think, rather, the lesson teaches a pupil to engage in critical thinking and articulate their own point of view. In this way we prepare children for life in modern Britain where different ideas and beliefs exist and rub alongside each other. It's ok to agree and it's ok to disagree, as long as you are disagreeing respectfully.

In a No Outsiders lesson the teacher does not give their opinion; we are not telling children what they must think or steering pupils down a predetermined path. So, what do you do when ideas are expressed in class that challenge inclusion? If we are teaching pupils to engage in debate and articulate opinions freely, we can't expect them to always articulate the opinions we may hope for. Furthermore, we can't create a culture where pupils are encouraged to agree and disagree but then tell a pupil, 'You can't say that!' Either we are truly welcoming different ideas, or we are not.

In this particular lesson on the first day in Y6 we used a No Outsiders assembly written to explore responses to the sudden appearance in September 2025 of St George's flags on roundabouts and lamp posts across the UK. The assembly started with an artist impression of a school building where the walls were made up of eight different flags. Pupils were asked to consider what message the artist was trying to convey and how this linked to our school.

'Why not just use one flag instead of eight?' was one question. The pupils were reassuring in their inclusive responses; the consensus appeared to be that the artist was saying everyone was welcome in her school and that's what we say here. As a follow-up task, pupils were given a blank version of the school outline to fill in with illustrations of their choice; they may choose to use flags or they may not; there was no direction give. Pupils then wrote a paragraph to explain the message behind their art. Most pupils were incredibly welcoming in their follow-up work, using a range of flags, rainbows, showing children who looked different, etc. However, in the mix of inclusion, one child drew a school with only St George's flags and wrote refugees were not allowed: 'The only people allowed in our school are people from Great Britain.'

As a teacher, how do you respond to this? Fortunately, I had delivered No Outsiders training to staff only days before this, so the teacher knew not to comment. The response is, 'Interesting!' I always start my No Outsiders training sessions by talking about creating the narrative in school which may contrast to the narrative outside. I cannot control the narrative outside the school gates. Of course that narrative may be inclusive and welcoming anyway. Pupils may be hearing messages of diversity and inclusion, in which case there is no need to worry. But what if they are not hearing positive messages about diversity and inclusion? What if they are hearing racist rhetoric from social media, YouTube, family or community members? I can't control that. I have absolutely no control over what pupils hear outside school gates. The place I can control the narrative is inside the school gates where everyone is welcome and that's what I will focus on.

The pupil in question is clearly hearing messages outside school that hit against our school culture of inclusion so all I can do is work with those ideas, accept that they exist and make clear the narrative inside the school.

I made a display to showcase all the beautiful responses to the assembly from across the school. I asked each class to send me two pieces of work, and I put them up in the centre of the school outside the hall. There was an explanation next to the display with a picture of the original art work:

> *'This image was created by Fliss who is an artist at Fledgling Education. Fliss used flags to make up the windows and walls in her school. Fliss says, "I live my life in colour, and this image is a celebration of that spirit." We were inspired by Fliss to create our own schools. In class, we discussed the importance of "everyone is welcome in our school" and what this looks like. There are no outsiders here.'*

The Year 6 classes went further and discussed the make-up of their classes. Each provided a breakdown which was added to the display. One read:

> *'Bosnian, German, Jamaican, Brazilian, Irish, Scottish, French, Chinese, Syrian, Lebanese, Iranian, Indian, British, Welsh, African, American, Australian, Gambian, Mexican, Barbadian. Muslim, Christian, Catholic, Hindu.*
>
> *We have autism, ADHD, allergies, birth marks, different sight, eczema, psoriasis, we stutter.*
>
> *We have beautiful brown skin, beautiful black skin, beautiful freckles, beautiful white skin.*
>
> *We have siblings and we don't. We have different families.*
>
> *We have accents.'*

Another class included the line, 'We are Christian, Catholic, Musim, Atheist and some of us are still searching and open.'

This is a great example of controlling the narrative inside the school. While we accept that other ideas exist and may be prevalent, in our school, we say everyone is welcome. The following week, Year 6 taught a No Outsiders lesson about refugees using the text 'The Island' by Armin Greder. In the book a stranger arrives on an island and is immediately mistrusted by the islanders who reject him because he is not like them. At the end of the story, the islanders send the man back to the sea, back to 'where he came from'. It's a shocking ending which provides a great opportunity for discussion around why the man might have come (we are not told this) and why the islanders treated him in this way. Where do these actions, these fears, originate from and what do we say at our school?

Following the No Outsiders lesson plan, the pupils wrote diary entries for characters in the book.

They could choose which character to give a voice to and could choose their characters' perspective. Interestingly, the pupil who a week before had written refugees were not welcome, now wrote a piece empathising with the refugee in the book. The pupil questioned why the islanders hated the man just because he came from a different country and furthermore about parents using the stranger to instil fear in their children. Again, the teacher made no comment, neither agreeing or disagreeing but complimenting the child on their empathy skills and imagination.

It appears that in the space of a week, a child has shifted in their attitudes towards refugees. Of course, they may not have changed their mind, it may be that they were writing in character, but at least that shows that they are able to see different points of view. These attitudes may change again and that's ok. The key is that pupils are being given space and opportunity to explore ideas and debate. In this way we nurture inclusion and prepare children for life in modern Britain.

Andrew Moffat works as PD Lead for Excelsior MAT in Birmingham.

The lesson plan referenced in this article is part of the No Outsiders scheme 'No Outsiders: We belong here' by Andrew Moffat (Speechmark, 2024)

Link to the flag assembly https://no-outsiders-assembly.blogspot.com/2025/08/flags.html

There is a new No Outsiders assembly published every week, free to access on the No Outsiders website www.no-outsiders.com

Case study question: How can schools balance teaching inclusion and respect with allowing pupils to express views that may challenge these values?

How Do Schools Implement Changes?

- How do we initiate the changes?
- How do we engage others to be part of the change?
- How do we sustain the change?

Kotter's (1995) model is also a well-known model in terms of leading and creating a culture of change and has increased in popularity within Education (Appelbaum et al., 2012). Kotter's model helps to clarify these questions above.

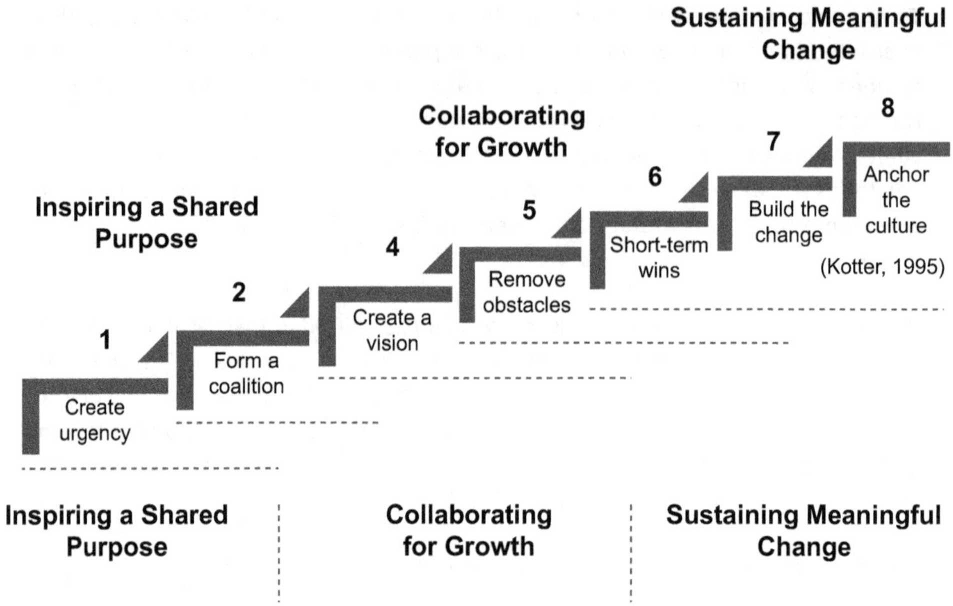

Figure 5.3 Adapted from Kotter's Eight-Step Change Model (1995)

The first three steps of Kotter's model are collectively referred to as 'Creating a Climate for Change'. These are the stages whereby the need for change is articulated, a coalition is formed, and it is then this group (particularly middle leaders) who will collaboratively create or refine the vision for the change and define the intended school change.

The second three steps of Kotter's model are collectively referred to as 'engaging and enabling the whole school community'. According to Kotter (1995), these are the stages whereby it is important to communicate the vision and talk about it every chance you get. It is important that the message and the language are always consistent among the coalition. In order to remove obstacles and create short-term wins, it is important that the high expectations and professional standards can be broken down into manageable and celebratory items to demonstrate ongoing success, towards the intended culture. The final two steps of Kotter's model are collectively referred to as 'implementing and sustaining the change'.

It is important in these stages to allow reflection and learning from any mistakes, so that the change can be sustained, but also so that it can mould to the context naturally. Kotter (1995) states that it is important to publicly recognise key members of your original change coalition and make sure the rest of the staff - new and existing - remembers their contributions. However, it is important to also recognise the wider school community, so everyone feels that they have been part of this successful change.

Case Study: St Matthew's Church of England Primary School, Redhill, Surrey

Kate Penfold, Head Teacher

WELCOME   Ẹ káàbọ̀   **வரவேற்கிறேன்**

We are proud of St Matthew's School – our inclusive, diverse, Church of England Primary School in the centre of Redhill. We are a two-form entry primary school; an academy in The Southwark Diocesan Board of Education Multi-Academy Trust. We have a nursery, primary classes for children aged 4–11 years and a special needs support centre for children with a diagnosis of ASD.

Together with Trust leaders, we have high expectations for all our children and work to ensure they make excellent progress from their starting points during their time with us. One of the key ways for us to do this is by building strong relationships with children and families. Induction is key to ensuring all in our diverse community feel a part of what we do; this induction is for staff and children.

To be able to serve our diverse community as best we can, we have spent time on a 'tour of beauty' of our area so that we can know, love and advocate for our area and those who live in it. Bespoke home visits also happen whenever any new families join our school. This could be ahead of a September start or at any point during the year. Being visible, accessible and open to parents and prospective parents is key to good partnership work for us. Our clear, strong ordinarily available provision offer and our pathway for children with English as an Additional Language are two strategies we use to cater for some of the largest groups in our diverse community.

We have staff that speak several different languages, use clear visuals and Google Translate where appropriate and make decisions based on need. These all impact how successfully our community works together. Overall, the biggest driver in ensuring our diverse community lives and works well together is our vision that we are here to 'Encourage one another and build one another up'.

Case study question: How do strong relationships with children, families and the local community support inclusion and help all pupils thrive?

A diverse school community is important not just for the reasons stated above but also because:

- This diverse culture provides the environment where young people can think critically and develop a well-rounded view of the world.
- It creates opportunities for different and or opposing views and experiences which go some way to build and develop emotional intelligence and resilience in children.
- This school culture introduces young people to idea of different perspectives. It teaches children how to listen to different points of view and that there can be different points of views which are not wrong.

Therefore, we can say that some of the benefits of teaching from a culturally diverse curriculum include:

- Young people feel seen and fully represented in the curriculum and supported by the school.
- Questions viewpoints, prejudices, and stereotypes.
- The creation of a culture of empathy and resilience - instilling this in young people.
- Providing a healthy environment in which to debate and discuss opposing views.
- Increasing pupil engagement.
- Decreasing pupil absence.

How to Implement Interventions with Diversity and Inclusion at the Core

To effectively promote an inclusive and diverse school, interventions should be intentional and evidence informed. Key principles and practical approaches include:

Evaluate the whole child through an equity lens. This should include pupil voice, family feedback and staff feedback to ensure interventions respond holistically to the child.

Interventions are most effective when all members of the school community are fully onboard, from senior leaders, teachers, support staff and governors. There is a shared responsibility and accountability for the outcomes.

Professional development should focus on unconscious bias so that adaptive teaching can be fully embedded. Allow and create time for staff reflection so that practice can evolve in response to pupils' needs.

Support such as mentoring, language development or wellbeing programmes should be framed positively and embedded into universal provision where possible to avoid marginalisation.

Create partnerships with families and local communities to help design interventions. This may include workshops, specialists or celebrating community knowledge within the school.

Inclusive interventions should be regularly reviewed for impact. Schools should be able to stop an intervention that does not improve engagement, belonging or outcomes for all learners.

Chapter Takeaways

Reflections

- Diversity must be embedded across the whole school and curricula, shaping pupils' sense of belonging, identity and possibility, rather than being treated as a tokenistic addition.
- When children see themselves and others reflected authentically in the curriculum, it broadens their understanding of who they can become, raises engagement and supports positive social and emotional development.
- Effective teaching recognises different starting points and lived experiences - looking at the young person holistically - using adaptive and responsive approaches to ensure all pupils can access and succeed within the curriculum.
- Diversification of the curriculum depends on a shared vision, professional learning - continuous professional development, community collaboration and ongoing evaluation to ensure impact on inclusion, engagement and outcomes for all learners.

Now Consider

- How diverse is your curriculum?
- How do you ensure all children are represented in school?
- In what ways does your curriculum and curricula offer diverse perspectives and opportunities?
- Consider using the diversity audit to assess your current curriculum.

Enhanced Provision and Ideas to Support Learning

- Curriculum Diversity audit - use a RAG-rated framework rather than overload.
- Diversify display boards.

- Include multi-cultural music.
- Multilingual signage around the school.
- Review resources, toys, role-play areas.
- Provide allocated time to implement and respond.
- Invite the local community to supplement learning – guest speakers, storytelling.
- Diversify books.
- Include translated texts/books for the languages in your school.
- Review scaffolding prompts – use multimodal approaches to reduce barriers.
- Link pupils with role-models and mentors from diverse backgrounds.
- Provide interventions for wellbeing or those who might feel marginalised.
- Create a 'working group' – a diversity lead.

Further Reading

- *The diverse curriculum* – Bennie Kara
- *Diversity, equity, inclusion and teaching* – Lucy Davies and Kulwinder Maude
- *Diversity in the Curriculum Toolkit* – curated by Diverse Educators, with articles by practitioners and links to curriculum diversity resources

Bibliography

Appelbaum, S., Habashy, S., Malo, J.-L. and Shafiq, H. (2012). 'Back to the future: Revisiting Kotter's 1996 change model'. *Journal of Management Development*, 31(8), 764–782. file:///C:/Users/Louise/Downloads/Back_to_the_future_Revisiting_Kotters_1996_change.pdf.

Biesta, G. (2021). *World-centred education: A view for the present*. London: Routledge.

Collins Dictionary. (2025). *Diversity*. https://www.collinsdictionary.com/dictionary/english/diversity.

Brett, P. and Brassington, T. (2023). 'Diversity, representation and curriculum inclusion', in M. Myatt, *The Curriculum: Gallimaufry to Coherence*. Carmarthen: Crown House Publishing, pp. 49–58.

Davis, L. (2025). 'Beyond the tick box: Diversity in the curriculum'. *Impact*, 25, 68–69.

Department for Education. (2025). *Persistent absence rates by school type, 2017/18 to 2024/25*. Explore Education Statistics. https://explore-education-statistics.service.gov.uk/find-statistics/pupil-absence-in-schools-in-england.

Department for Education. (2025). 'Schools, pupils and their characteristics, Academic year 2024/25 – Explore education statistics'. *Explore Education Statistics*. https://explore-education-statistics.service.gov.uk/find-statistics/school-pupils-and-their-characteristics/2024-25.

Department for Education. (2025). *Curriculum and Assessment Review Final Report*. DfE. https://www.gov.uk/government/publications/curriculum-and-assessment-review-final-report.

Impact. (2025). 'Beyond the tick box: Diversity in the curriculum'. *Impact*. https://my.chartered.college/impact_article/beyond-the-tick-box-diversity-in-the-curriculum/.

Kara, B. (2024). *The diverse curriculum*. Thousand Oaks, CA: SAGE Publications, Incorporated.

Kotter, J.P. (1995). 'Leading change: Why transformation efforts fail'. *Harvard Business Review*, 73(2), 59–67.

Lomax, N., Norman, P., Rees, P. and Stillwell, J. (2019). 'The impacts of international migration on the UK's ethnic populations'. *Journal of Ethnic and Migration Studies*, 46(1), 177–199. file:///C:/Users/Louise/Downloads/LomaxWohlandReesNorman2019JEMSPaper.pdf.

McKeating, C. (2022). 'Representation is important for all children to see themselves in learning tools, books and have role models in the home, school and around them'. In M. Myatt, *The Curriculum: Gallimaufry to Coherence*. Carmarthen: Crown House Publishing.

Munoz, Dr. M. (2025). 'A spotlight on… Decolonising the Curriculum'. University of Liverpool. https://www.liverpool.ac.uk/media/livacuk/centre-for-innovation-in-education/staff-guides/decolonising-the-curriculum/decolonising-the-curriculum.pdf.

Oxford English Dictionary. (n.d.). 'Diversity noun'. *Oxford English Dictionary*, https://www.oed.com/dictionary/diversity_n?tl=true.

Pearson. (2020). 'Diversity and inclusion in schools'. https://www.opinium.com/wp-content/uploads/2021/03/diversity-and-inclusion-in-schools-report-Pearson.pdf.

6
Skills for Life

Ensuring that all young people have the skills necessary to thrive and lead fulfilling lives long after their education has finished must be one of the essential aims of education.

Pre reading Reflection Questions

- What are the skills needed for the future?
- To what extent are you aware of the skills children in **your** school need to be successful in their future?
- How do you currently cater for these particular skills within your school/setting?

Essential Skills for Life

There are seven essential life skills that are widely recognised as the key to thriving, rather than simply surviving: in school, in workplaces, and in healthy relationships (Galinksy, 2010). Galinsky categorises these skills as: focus and self-control, communication, problem-solving, critical thinking, empathy and perspective-taking, self-directed learning and resilience in coping with stress. We will consider each in more detail:

1. Focus and Self-Control (Executive Function): This focuses on an individual's ability to manage their emotions; maintain focus and attention; and stay committed to goals - skills that are fundamental to learning in education and everyday responsibilities in general life and when employed to work.
2. Communication: Being able to clearly express ideas and listen to others effectively are essential skills which enable individuals to collaborate; building strong relationships, both personally and professionally.
3. Problem-Solving: It is important for an individual to be able to identify challenges and then be able to explore these by developing effective solutions. This is a life skill that is critically important for navigating life's challenges.
4. Critical Thinking: We need to be able to objectively analyse information to then make informed decisions; especially in unfamiliar circumstances.

DOI: 10.4324/9781003624004-6

5. Empathy & Perspective: When we can listen to and value other people's feelings and viewpoints this will help them to build successful social connections and develop their own appreciation of diversity – a skill that is important in our ever-changing society.
6. Self-Directed Learning (a sense of curiosity): When an individual has a genuine interest in a topic or subject, which is then nurtured by those around them, they are more likely to become a curious thinker – taking initiatives in their own learning and building an ability to be able to adapt to new situations. In turn, this can form a secure platform for lifelong growth.
7. Resilience and Coping with Stress (Adaptability): Managing emotions and recovering from setbacks is important for children (and adults). This skill of resilience enables individuals to handle life's challenges with confidence and move forward and learn from failures. This is particularly important for disadvantaged children who are reported to be less resilient than their more advantaged peers, due to their early-life experiences.

Working Memory and Life Skills

Working memory, the brain's short-term mental workspace, plays a vital role in everyday functioning. It underpins essential life skills, detailed above, and is essential for enabling emotional regulation by temporarily holding and manipulating information needed for immediate tasks. Whether following instructions, comprehending new material, or managing daily activities, our working memory supports the execution of complex behaviours.

Daniel Willingham's model of working memory (2017), which builds upon previous models (Baddeley and Hitch, 1974), describes working memory as a system with limited capacity but which is essential for conscious thought and active mental processing (Willingham, 2017). Functioning as a bridge between sensory input and long-term memory, working memory temporarily holds and manipulates information as it is being processed. For learning to happen, this information must be successfully transferred into long-term memory, highlighting the importance of instructional practices that manage cognitive load and intentionally direct student attention. In other words, for the new information to be stored successfully in someone's brain or long-term memory, the brain needs to make meaningful connections with the information so it can be accessed later.

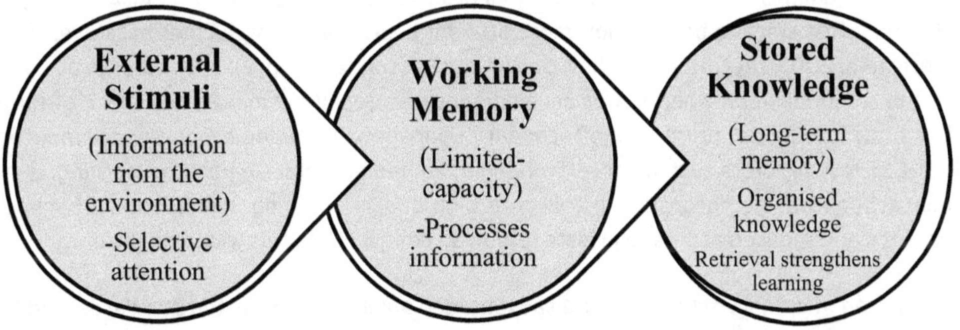

Figure 6.1 A simplified model of attention, working memory and long-term memory

(Adapted from Willingham 2009)

Moving Forward - Children of the Future

When thinking about skills for the future, we need to consider where children and young people are now so that practitioners can meet these children at their current stage of education.

David Ausubel (an American psychologist), who specialised in cognitive science, framed a theory of learning, called the 'Theory of Meaningful Learning'. This theory's central premise is that 'what a learner already knows is the most influential factor in acquiring new knowledge' (Akpan and Kennedy, 2020).

He argued that meaningful learning occurs when new information is deliberately connected to existing understanding rather than memorised in isolation. Through this process, new concepts are integrated into an organised network of prior knowledge. To support this integration, Ausubel introduced the use of 'advanced organisers' (2020, cited in Bryce and Brown, 2023). These introductory frameworks help learners bridge gaps between what they know and what they are about to learn. It is essential that we look at all children through a long-term lens rather than considering the impact of short-termism in education so that we can build their pathway of life.

In a previous chapter we discussed how a child's home life, upbringing and life events also shape how they respond to what happens in the classroom. Bronfenbrenner (1986) (see Figure 6.2) captures these different layers which influence a child's life in his Ecological Systems Theory. The framework helps us to understand human development by examining how individuals interact with their surrounding environments.

Bronfenbrenner's Ecological Systems Theory model illustrates the strong connection between a child's early years home life and how ready and well-equipped young people are to enter the work force. It emphasises that a young person's development is shaped by multiple layers of environment, from immediate settings such as school and home life to broad cultural forces, and changes over time and these filters through to their next stage of life. Interestingly, socio-economic inequalities widen as they progress through school (Fernstein 2003).

These inequalities widen markedly as pupils progress through school, with disadvantaged children often starting behind their more affluent peers and falling further back over time (Fernstein, 2003). According to Shay, Shavit and Sasson (2025, p. 2), gaps emerge as early as the reception year, where lower developmental scores are common, and these disparities grow throughout primary and secondary education, becoming especially pronounced at GCSE level. Factors such as poverty, hunger, limited parental support for learning, unequal school funding, inconsistent access to high-quality teaching, higher rates of school absence and reduced access to private tuition all contribute to this widening divide.

By the end of primary school, fewer disadvantaged pupils meet expected standards, and by GCSEs they are far less likely to achieve strong results in English and Mathematics. These

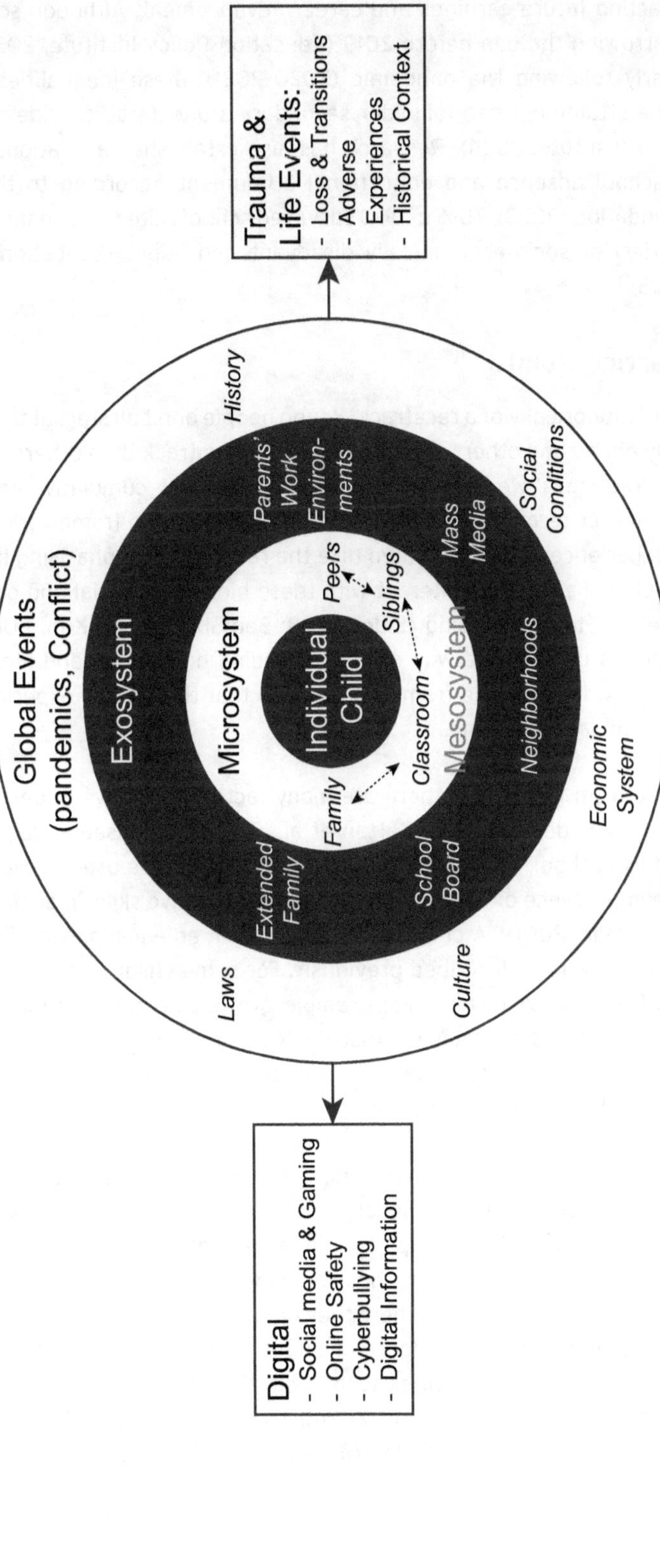

Figure 6.2 Bronfenbrenner's Ecological Systems Theory

are differences that significantly affect progression to university and, later, outcomes in the workplace, impacting future earnings and career advancement. Although some progress was made in narrowing the gap before 2019 (Education Policy Institute, 2024), in recent years, particularly following the pandemic (2020–2021), these inequalities have deepened, leaving the attainment gap for older secondary students at its widest in a decade (Education Policy Institute, 2024). Research has also established a relationship between disadvantage, school absence and educational attainment According to the Education Endowment Foundation (2023), 75% of 300 surveyed schools cited attendance as the main attainment barrier for socio-economically disadvantaged pupils (Education Endowment Foundation, 2023).

Different Starting Points

We could think metaphorically of a racetrack. Young people don't all start at the same place, some are slightly ahead and others start further along the track than others. When we are considering this 'racetrack' we are referring to the concept of 'cumulative advantage and disadvantage'. Another term for this metaphor is the 'life course framework' which views health and life experiences as a continuum (like the racetrack), emphasising how early-life events and cumulative exposures interact with these biological, social and environmental factors to shape long-term wellbeing (Elder, 1998; Ben-Shlomo and Kuh, 2002). The 'life course framework' is ultimately a way of understanding how health and life experiences develop over time. At its core, the framework argues that these early experiences matter because they accumulate over time.

What we can take from this is that there are many factors that have a long-term impact on young people's skill development (Cattan et al., 2022). Any disadvantage starts long before a child starts school. Indeed, 'skills beget skills' – a phrase used by Heckman when emphasising the importance of both cognitive and noncognitive skills in achieving success in the future (Heckman, 2000). A child's start in life is not an equal playing field – think of the analogy of the racetrack described previously. For some children, starting their life in poverty will only lead to more poverty. For example, growing up in poverty will lead to gaps in their cultural capital and schemas or Ausbel's 'Advanced organisers' – and this will, in turn, impede their learning and development. As educators, we need to help level this 'playing field' or 'racetrack' as much as possible.

Not all young people have the same experiences and opportunities, and it is these experiences which affect a child's cultural schema. They do not, for example, have the same access to extra-curricular activities, trips and life experiences such as visits to cities, the theatre, museums, the coast or abroad. These activities usually have both direct and indirect costs for parents and for schools, where they are often included as part of an extended school day. Unsurprisingly, there is evidence of a direct link between household income and participation in extra-curricular activities such as sports clubs, and clubs for hobbies, arts and music (Donnelly et al., 2019; Robinson, 2024). Access to extra-curricular activities also varies by geography (Robinson, 2024). In order to face these issues in schools (and level the playing field) leaders need to essentially 'poverty proof' the school day. We will consider strategies to do this later in the chapter.

Skills for an Unknown Future

Let us first consider what the research states are the skills needed for the future. The National Foundation for Educational Research (Bocock, Scott and Hillary, 2025) report has identified a set of skills that are relied upon today across the workforce, but which will be in even greater demand by 2035.

Young people's skill development is often seen as the responsibility of the post-16 education system, with input from employers. For example, the previous government's 'Skills for Jobs' white paper laid out reforms to the post-16 education system but made minimal reference to what happens before 16 (DfE, 2021). In the same way, the primary focus of Skills England (2025) appears to be on the post-16 skills pipelines. The report mentions the requirements for upskilling for new technologies, sustainable energy and advanced manufacturing but does not provide any detail on how skills are taught in schools. Instead, it focuses on what happens after compulsory schooling, how to bridge gaps and how to make post-16 pathways more flexible and responsive to employer needs. The only specific references are made to foundational skills-such as English and maths, taught in primary and secondary schools. The report makes the point that 'low standards in basic skills limit progression into apprenticeships and technical training' (Skills England, 2025).

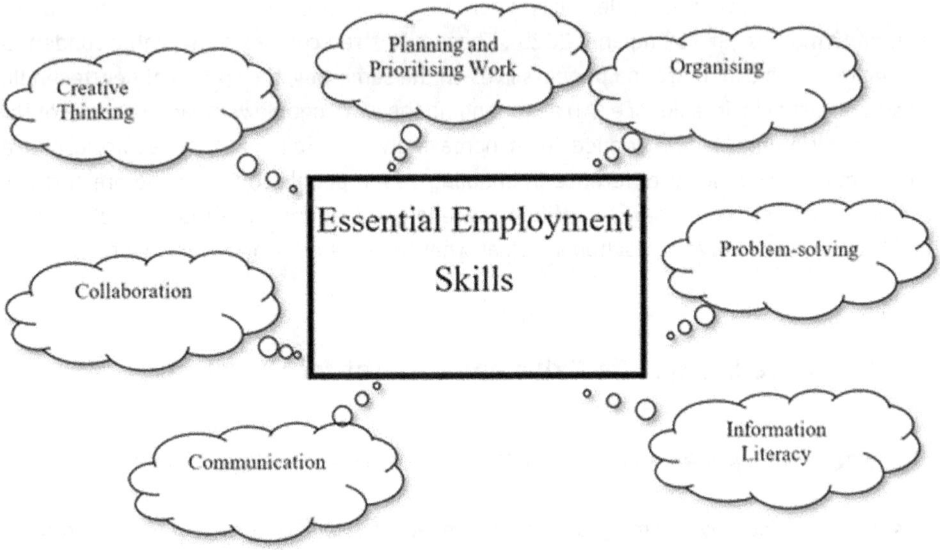

Figure 6.3 Essential employment skills

(Bocock, Scott and Hillary, 2025)

Employer-reported skills gaps suggest many employers are not convinced that the education system is producing young adults with strong EES (IFF Research, 2023). Research by Bocock, Scott and Hillary (2024) suggests these skill gaps are likely to become increasingly acute between now and 2035. Children's cognitive and behavioural development are deeply connected, with early abilities in both areas strongly influencing later outcomes. Families and the education system play a vital role in building this foundation, helping children develop the skills they need as they move towards adulthood and the workforce. To meet the demands of a changing economy and support long-term growth, the government should adopt a lifelong, 'cradle to grave' approach to skills development - one that nurtures a balanced mix of cognitive, behavioural, technical, and subject-specific skills at every stage of life.

Lifelong Learning as a Core Life Skill

Certainly, in 2026 the thinking that education ends when young people graduate or finish their time at school is an outdated view. Dylan Williams' 'always learning' theory (2009), focuses on the importance of adaptation and feedback and this is true in all aspects of education and life. We believe that 'lifelong learning' has to be the mantra to live by. When an individual is committed to lifelong learning they are not in a race to success; they are curious and self-motivated in their pursuit of personal development - a characteristic that children need to be successful adults.

The world of work faces rapid change and the need to learn new skills and new ways of working are essential to keep up with this pace of rapid change. It's hardly surprising that there is an increase in nano and micro learning courses (Peck, 2025). Time seems to be getting quicker. Students want to gain their qualifications and training in a shorter amount of time. The government even reports that employers are interested in shortening the duration of apprenticeships to give greater flexibility where skills and competence could be developed in less than 12 months (Skills England, 2025). These bite-sized courses offer highly condensed information which can fit around people's lives. In the same way, the spread of new technologies such as artificial intelligence (AI) are changing the ways people work and because of this we will see different skill sets needed. In an increasingly uncertain and complex world, education can make a significant difference in enabling young people to thrive. We are certainly in an era characterised by new scientific knowledge. It is appropriate that school curricula should continue to evolve and schools look at what they are offering their students.

Case Study: Life Skills and a Thirst for Knowledge

Head Teacher, Kate Penfold - St Matthew's CE Primary School, Redhill

As a diverse, inclusive primary school, we believe it is our role to develop children's thirst for knowledge, life skills and to provide them with experiences they wouldn't otherwise have.

Community involvement is an essential part of our curriculum as we celebrate local and national festivals and traditions, learning new skills to enable the children to take an active role society. We have strong partnerships in our local community organisations including: the church, tennis club, other schools and businesses and links further afield. We take time to build excellent working relationships with organisations that will build our children's skills for life. One example of this is our link with Prept Foundation for food education who offer immersive cooking experiences in the classroom and on a farm! As well as modelling healthy relationships with food, they teach front of house skills, eye contact, how to welcome newcomers and set a table. They do all this to enhance 'confidence and aspirations by enabling children to see the value of good presentation, communication and social skills, as well as recognising the importance of sitting down and enjoying food together'.

We want our children to be aspirational for themselves so that they can have successful futures. Another key way we do this is through our wide and varied programme of extended learning activities. We believe that participation in clubs, visits and other activities are key elements of a well-rounded education, benefiting children's confidence, self-esteem, resilience, social skills and aspirations.

Visits to places of interest, both local and further afield, and residential trips are an integral part of the curriculum as is our extensive extra-curricular programme - clubs that take place at lunchtime or after school including choir, sports clubs, gardening, homework support, cooking and art all provided by qualified staff, free of charge so all are welcome.

Our commitment to take every child camping and for every child to perform on the stage at a theatre every other year during their primary education are also ways we demonstrate the value of wider skills. Where is resilience and stickability needed more than when the spotlight is on you on the stage or when you are working with your group to put up a tent for the first time . . . in the rain!

All of these experiences serve to show children what opportunities there are available for them in society and start them on the journey of building the required skills. Children leave St Matthew's School confident having been part of a close school community where they are known well, their gifts and talents are nurtured and celebrated and their aspirations are stretched.

Case study question: How do the experiences and opportunities provided at our school help children develop the confidence, resilience and social skills they will need in the wider world?

Skills for Life through the Skills Builder Framework

The Skills Builder Universal Framework provides a benchmark to track this progress. This framework supports teachers in planning for these skills and, further still, measuring the progress against these skills.

Skills Builder passionately believes that: '*One day, everyone will build the essential skills to succeed*' (Skills Builder, 2026). They support the belief that essential skills are the foundation of effective learning in the classroom, improving academic achievement, perseverance and self-belief. Skills Builder focuses on eight key skills for successful life and aspires for all children to develop and demonstrate these throughout their education and into adult life. The eight skills are: Listening, Speaking, Problem-Solving, Creativity, Adapting, Planning, Leadership and Teamwork.

Through cutting-edge research, The Skills Builder Universal Framework has made it possible to focus on key skills throughout different phases of life, supporting the most disadvantaged people at each stage of their life journey. They do this through teaching, learning and the ability to measure these essential skills. The five areas of focus are:

1. Pre-school education
2. The school years (EYFS to key stage 4)
3. Apprenticeships, college and university education
4. Early careers support
5. Mid-career development

Take a moment to consider the following questions

- How can education at all levels support the skills transition to ensure that no one is left behind?
- What are the particular skills the pupils and students you work with need for their future?

Case Study: Careers and Disadvantaged Students

James Faulkner - Great Baddow High School

Our aim at Great Baddow High School is to fully prepare all of our students for their choices at 14, 16 and 18, as well as for working life beyond further and/or higher education. This includes raising their aspirations, awareness and self-esteem through a varied careers programme that facilitates contact with employers, universities, colleges, training providers and other organisations.

We believe that one of the biggest barriers for some students is their ability to access workplace and further education experiences, whether due to transport concerns or a lack of family links. We therefore feel that the most effective way to support all our students, but particularly our disadvantaged students, is to provide as many of these experiences as possible within school as well as directly in a workplace.

Unlike traditional work experience placements, which typically involve two weeks in a workplace and often rely heavily on family connections and access to transport, we run a hybrid approach. Students still complete a traditional placement over two days, but the remainder is delivered through school-led experiences. These include school-organised trips for all students and in-school virtual work experience, allowing them to access workplaces and industries they might otherwise be unable to engage with.

Our annual careers fair brings together over 40 exhibitors from universities, apprenticeship providers and employers. Hosting this event on our school site ensures that all students have accessible and equitable exposure to a wide range of possible pathways without the need for complex travel arrangements or family support. We have found that disadvantaged students having so much contact with higher education providers at such a young age in Year 9 had greatly raised the student aspirations.

Disadvantaged students often prefer non-traditional post-16 pathways, such as apprenticeships or vocational courses. Prioritising them for early careers interviews enables us to support them effectively through 1-to-1 workshops focused on applications and apprenticeship processes. This information also allows us to plan targeted school trips to external open days for students who would otherwise be unable to attend.

Careers events

Students have access to a dedicated careers event each year aimed at enhancing their aspirations and understanding of their paths after leaving Great Baddow High School. Each year will have a different event tailored to the changing needs of our students. These include but are not limited to:

Year 7 – 'What's My Job?'
Aimed at widening students understanding of different jobs roles and challenging stereotypes. A 'What's My Job' event will let all of Year 7 meet employees from a range of career sectors to find out what their roles involves and the education and training that was required to get there.

Year 8 - 'Take Your Child to Work Day'
Nothing beats first-hand experience of the workplace. On our "Take Your Child to Work Day" we hope that all students will be able to organise a suitable day's experience with a parent, relative or someone you know well to be able to go into a work place.

Year 9 - Careers Fair
The annual Great Baddow High School careers fair is always a success with both students and parents alike. With over 50 stalls from a wide range of employment sectors, as well as universities and other training providers the fair is an amazing opportunity for students to gain a massive number of employer encounters. The fair is open to all Year 9–13 but is particularly useful for our Year 9 students as they approach their GCSE options for them to open their eyes to all the paths open to them and how to best prepare themselves to take them.

Year 9 – Options Evening
As our Year 9 students approach the time for picking their GCSE options for the following years our Options Evening gives all students and parents a chance to meet and discuss with all the subject areas what the course involves and the skills developed and required to succeed in it. Teachers will be able to go into greater detail what all their subjects have to offer and give honest and personalised advice to each student as to whether that subject is a good fit for them.

Year 10 – Interview Day
To start our preparations for our students to enter the world of work we have a Year 10 Interview Day. Students are not required to wear their school uniform and instead are encouraged to come in dressed to impress for their interviews with real local employers. Students have the whole day off timetable to go over polishing their CV and interview techniques. They then each get a one-to-one interview with a real industry employer to get first-hand experience in what a real interview will be like. Students then get feedback on how they did, with pointers on how to improve before each visiting employer picks their best candidates who would get the job.

Year 11 – Sixth Form Open Evening
As students start to look to the future and the different paths to take, we hope many will return to us for their level 3 studies. At our Sixth Form Open Evening, students and their parents get the chance to meet and discuss the courses and qualifications on offer in the Great Baddow High School Sixth Form, and the skills developed and required to succeed in it. Teachers will be able to go into greater detail what all their subjects have to offer and give honest and personalised advice to each student as to whether that subject is a good fit for them.
Year 11 – Apprenticeship Workshop

For those students who wish to start apprenticeship training at 16, there will be a workshop where they can find out more about apprenticeships and help to find out where and how to apply. Further support will be available as the year progresses.

Year 12 – Work Experience

At the end of Year 12 all our students spend two weeks gaining first-hand work experience in the industry of their choice. Students are encouraged to arrange their own placement with the support of the school to ensure they get an experience right for them. We check in with all students during their placements, to ensure they are enjoying their placement and getting all that they can from it.

Year 13 – Futures Day – UCAS and Apprenticeship Workshops

Futures day gives our Year 13 students a day off timetable to prepare for their future after Great Baddow High School. This includes an inspirational talk from Peter Dale, former Cambridge student, and a well-respected speaker. Students are then given guidance in either working on their UCAS forms for university applications or taking part in job and career sessions.

Careers Sixth Sense Lectures

All Sixth Form students have a termly talk from an external speaker, including independent careers advisors and guest speakers. The talks are aimed to provide students with useful information and advice on how to move forward with their post-sixth form plans.

By offering such a broad and varied set of experiences within school, we can ensure that all students receive vital information and opportunities needed to make informed decisions about their futures

Case study question: How does providing accessible, in-school and workplace career experiences help raise aspirations and remove barriers for disadvantaged students?

Why Is Resilience Important?

Resilience is the ability to bounce back when something has not gone quite to plan, and this happens a lot. We have seen this over the last few years with the outbreak of the pandemic in 2020. Life can be unpredictable. Arguably, young people are coping with so much in their lives from social media to peer pressure and school pressures. They need the right tools in order to succeed and be able to pick themselves up, and the ability to be resilient is an essential character trait for success. In the last few years, statistics show that one in five children and young people aged eight to 25 had a mental health condition (YoungMinds, 2025). This number has been rising since 2017, most notably in the 17-19 age group (YoungMinds, 2025). How do we help foster this resilience in young people today - especially for the most disadvantaged students?

Resilience is certainly something that can be taught and developed within a child's education. A young person's growth mindset can grow and expand, but only within the right conditions. Carol Dweck, a psychologist, who has written a lot about this notion of 'growth mindset' states that a 'person's intelligence or talent will not necessarily lead to success, it's their mindset which helps them achieve' (Dweck, 1999). Being resilient is one of the most valuable tools a young person can have in their own 'tool kit' - when schools provide the environment to help a young person's resilience grow, they are building the future foundations for this resilience to be used later in life.

How Can Schools Help Foster Resilience in Schools?

By being aware, recognising who are the children who need to build resilience and looking for ways in which to help them foster this within your school and classroom, the impact will have effective and lasting results for the young people.

Activities include:

1. Encouraging the children and young people to take risks: try to not 'fix' things for them. Sometimes letting the children have a go but not achieving the desired end result, even though you know how to do it, builds independence. They face the challenge and attempt the 'problem' themselves. Praising the effort is useful and shows the children that it's okay to not get it right the first time. Things do not always go to plan in life and so provide the environment for children when they are young to learn that it's okay to 'fail'. This way also shows acceptance of mistakes and losses.
2. Encourage independence: Actively ask children and young people what their next steps are, this helps build self-sufficiency and encourages them to think of their own solutions rather than just stepping in and solving the problem for them. Ask the children and young people what they think the answer is, what they could do next and what the solution might be.
3. Praise effort: Praising the effort spent on something, rather than always praising the accomplishment, shows young people that they don't always have to achieve something or accomplish something. They will grow to think that they must only have to be talented at something to be successful and so be afraid of failure. By praising the effort, this is what will help them truly succeed in life and deal with difficulties.
4. Discuss and name the emotion: Part of being resilient is learning to handle and manage our emotions. In order to do this, we need to teach children the different emotions and name them. Find opportunities to talk about emotions and allow students to express themselves. For example, when reading a novel in an English lesson, encourage students to explore the feelings of the characters and discuss how they might feel. This will encourage empathy.

5. Promote a positive mindset: Model to the children how you are thinking optimistically about something. It might be something that happens in the class - show the children how to focus on the positive rather than the negative in any situation which arises.
6. It is good to ask for help when needed: Explain to your students you are always available to be asked for help. Even though it is good to have a go first, as the teacher you can help if they really do need help.

We must prepare our young people for the opportunities and challenges which lay ahead, and this has to start now, as early as possible.

What to consider:

- Conduct a skills audit of the curriculum. To what extent are the following skills developed in your classroom and school: listening, speaking, problem-solving, creativity, staying positive, aiming high, leadership and teamwork?
- Look for opportunities where these skills are already entwined into the lessons. Where are there gaps?
- Are there opportunities for children to be exposed to these skills in the wider curricula of the school?

Using a skills audit (found in Chapter 8) it is possible to evaluate the extent to which key transferable skills are taught and embedded through classroom teaching, the wider curriculum and whole-school opportunities. These skills include:

- listening skills
- speaking skills
- problem-solving skills
- creative thinking skills and creativity
- staying positive (resilience)
- aiming high (aspirations and perseverance)
- leadership
- teamwork (collaboration skills)

What Else Needs to Be Considered?

Artificial Intelligence

Over the last few years, we have seen an explosion of AI features which are readily available to us. This is not just in the world of work but rather it is affecting many areas of our lives, including education.

A quick trawl through job listings highlights the huge increase in AI jobs now available and the need for AI talent is rapidly growing. For instance, recent figures reveal a sharp rise in the share of job advertisements mentioning AI (Yanatma, 2025). 'In major European economics, the share of GenAI-related job postings is more than in the 12 months to March 2025' (Yanatma, 2025). Furthermore, the skills needed by workers which are necessary for developing these AI systems has 'almost tripled as a share of employment in less than a decade' (Yanatma, 2025). But, the lack of AI skills could be viewed as a barrier, which varies across different areas (Department for Education, 2025). Certainly, how we integrate artificial intelligence into our classrooms is going to be on the agenda going forward.

The Department for Education (DfE) is investing £45 million to ensure that schools are adequately digitally connected to eliminate any digital divide (Department for Education, 2025). As well as this, the DfE has announced a further £1million of funding to help build AI tools that will help to reduce teacher workload and will help to incorporate AI tools in our classrooms (Department for Education, 2025).

How can AI be integrated into schools?

- Model how AI can be used explaining the ethical considerations. Explain how it can be used to assist with learning.
- Build in learning opportunities where AI can be used and teach how to use it safely as a tool.
- Use real-world examples to show the risks and teach children how to evaluate AI.
- Use AI as a motivational tool.

Key skills that AI can help nurture:

- Evaluate what they have read and seen - develop critical thinking.
- Consider ethics and be ethically aware.
- Promote a reflective dialogue - see AI as a partner not and craft questions to delve deeper.

AI is here to stay, and future-ready students will need both broad and specialised knowledge such as knowing how to apply skills such as artificial intelligence. Students will need to draw upon a broad range of skills, including cognitive and meta-cognitive skills - for example, critical thinking, creative thinking, learning to learn and self-regulation; social and emotional skills such as empathy, self-efficacy and collaboration; and practical and physical skills (e.g. using new information and communication technology devices). Addressing these future skills needed is likely to require planning and a strategic approach in our education system.

In the report 'Building Foundations' by the National Foundation for Education Research (NFER) (Bocock, del Pozo Segura and Hillary, 2025) they make the recommendation that 'schools would benefit from access to a clear model or framework they can use to develop students' EES within and beyond the curriculum' (NFER, 2025). This is so that schools can ensure children and young people are being taught a range of transferable skills. This is because there is clear evidence that high-quality education right from the early years can impact the development of essential/transferable skills (Ofsted, 2024). Evidence in this paper suggests the skills gaps in the early years are predictive of skills gaps at the end of childhood.

In January 2026 the government announced that they were in the process of developing and rolling out the introduction of AI-powered tutoring tools for schools, with a particular focus on supporting pupils from disadvantaged backgrounds (GOV.UK, 2026). They estimate that around 450,000 pupils in years 9–11 would benefit from the scheme each year. Their aim is to have this in place by the end of 2027 (GOV.UK, 2026). This is due to data persistently showing attainment gaps between disadvantaged students and their peers. The aim of this AI programme is to bring equity to tuition; research shows that 1:1 tuition can accelerate progress rapidly; however, due to financial barriers tuition is mainly accessed by wealthier families.

Financial Education

Financial education is a key skill that children need as they grow up – the ability to budget and manage their finances is essential to being independent and successful in adulthood.

Although many of these topics are often integrated into secondary school curricula, such as citizenship, life skills and mathematics, there is a growing movement advocating for comprehensive financial literacy lessons to begin in primary schools to reduce financial anxiety and improve decision-making. In primary schools, financial education generally focuses on recognising money, performing simple calculations, understanding the importance of saving and learning the value of planning ahead, while secondary education builds on this foundation by introducing more complex concepts, including interest rates, credit and debt management, insurance and pension planning. Financial literacy education became part of the National Curriculum in 2014 for Key Stages 3 and 4 as part of citizenship education but it is not currently mandatory in primary schools; however, many schools are now building forward-thinking curriculums with money management as a key part, along with careers education.

Overall, levels of financial knowledge remain low, with only 19% of respondents able to answer all three core questions on interest, inflation and risk correctly, and a mere 3% successfully answering all five of the LFBF's own financial capability questions (The London Foundation for Banking and Finance, 2025).

Like all areas of education there are barriers that need to be raised to allow for the effective implementation of financial literacy education within schools' curriculums. These barriers include:

- Limited time in an already overstretched curriculum.
- Limited awareness among school decision-makers and a lack of robust impact data, both of which reduce its prioritisation within the curriculum.

- Limited training, budgets and resources to support the upskilling of teachers who may lack the confidence and subject knowledge required to deliver financial literacy education effectively.
- A possible disconnection between financial literacy learning at school and at home, shaped by cultural sensitivities and varying levels of parental financial literacy, which together undermine the consistency and effectiveness of delivery.

Young Enterprises conducted a report on 'Making the classroom count' (Young Enterprise, 2025). Within the report they focus on five areas of development to ensure a well-rounded financial literacy curriculum in schools. These are detailed below with the impact highlighted in Figure 6.5.

Take a moment to consider how financial literacy is taught across the ages within your school?

1. Curriculum – Inclusion and visibility in the national curriculum and local skills plans
2. Accountability – Clear inspection and performance measurements
3. Guidance – Cohesive and trusted content and guidance
4. Awareness – Recognise the importance of financial education in schools
5. Resources – Funding and capacity to deliver financial education

In the new proposed National Curriculum in England, financial education is being strengthened through mandatory inclusion in secondary school subjects such as Citizenship and Maths, alongside expanding initiatives for primary schools (GOV.UK, 2025). A national target aimed to reach more children by 2030, emphasising practical money skills, parent engagement, and addressing the current financial literacy shortfall.

Starting financial education early is an essential skill because children's money attitudes begin to form by age seven (Money and Pensions Service, 2025), making it important to introduce money concepts even from pre-school. With the ever-decreasing use of cash and the growing use of online banking it's important to help children to understand the concept of money, spending and debt alongside investment and money management. Practical learning should combine classroom lessons with real-world application, such as school savings banks or budget management activities. Engaging parents is also crucial, as financial education is more effective when learning continues at home.

Technology – Friend or Foe, It's a Skill for Modern Life

The last decade has seen an exponential rise in the use of technology by both students and teachers alike. Whether children are using technology as part of their school work, to support learning at home, playing games online, connecting with family and friends though social media or carrying out everyday tasks like searching the news, the need for digital literacy is increasingly becoming an essential life skill.

Moreover, as artificial intelligence becomes more advanced, digital skills will continue to feature prominently in the future of the workplace that today's children will enter in adulthood. Whether we love it or hate it, technology is here to stay and it is important that we educate children about this essential life skill; which when used correctly has a positive impact on learning. We have previously touched upon the change in employment over the last 20 years and it's important that technology and safety around this are life skills that are taught to all children from a very young age.

First, let's start with the barriers that technology lays. In a technological world we are all too aware of the negative media surrounding the internet; whether that is social media, screen time or deep fakes.

As part of mandatory RHSE (Relationship, Health and Sex Education) in primary and secondary schools, pupils are taught about online safety in an age-appropriate way. It is important too that parents and carers are involved in this education as it changes rapidly and often young people are ahead of the curve.

Physical impacts:

- Decrease in motor skills in young children
- Poor posture
- Lack of sleep so less able to focus on learning
- Blue light can use disruption to sleep
- Headaches and eye strain

Emotional and mental health impacts:

- Anxiety
- Lower self esteem
- Depression
- Lack of ability to regulate when screen time is removed
- Shortened attention span and need to immediate results

Negative impacts of technology on children and young people.

Social and behavioural impacts:

- Lack of face-to-face interactions and communication
- Reduced social skills
- Addictive behaviours
- Increase in ADHD
- Increase in bullying due to being 'hidden' behind a screen

Academic and cognitive impacts:

- Reduced attention span – impacting attention in school
- Reduced problem-solving skills
- Less resilience when faced with challenged
- Negative impact on vocabulary due to less conversation

Safety risks and their impacts:

- Exposure to innapropriate images
- Exposure to violent or explicit images
- Cyber bullying
- Negative impacts of social media
- Exploitation

Figure 6.4 Negative impact of technology

Take a moment to consider the apps and games that children in your class access. Are they all age appropriate and within them are there safety features to protect children?

In primary school, children are taught that people may behave differently online, including pretending to be someone they are not, and that the same principles apply to online and face-to-face relationships, particularly the importance of respect for others. They learn the rules and principles for staying safe online, including how to recognise risks, harmful content and contact, how to report concerns, how to think critically about online friendships and sources of information and how information and data are shared and used online. In secondary school, children are taught about their rights, responsibilities and opportunities online, the importance of not sharing content they would not want passed on or personal material sent to them by others, and where to get support to report material or manage online issues. They also learn about the impact of viewing harmful content, how sexually explicit material such as pornography can present a distorted picture of sexual behaviour, that sharing or viewing indecent images of children (including those created by children) is a serious criminal offence with severe penalties, and how information and data are generated, collected, shared and used online.

There are numerous charities and groups that support online safety including the Breck Foundation, childnet, and Thinkyouknow. The UK Online Safety Act 2025 places an emphasis on child safety, requiring that platforms prevent children from accessing pornography and other harmful content such as bullying, self-harm and eating disorder material. Social media and pornographic sites must implement highly effective age assurance platforms and have a legal duty of care to proactively remove illegal content and prevent children from encountering it. The Act also places responsibilities on search engines to filter harmful content, including the use of safe search defaults. Looking ahead, regulators expect platforms to move beyond initial compliance and demonstrate measurable, substantive improvements in online safety. With some countries introducing social media bans for under 16s, it's clear that this is being taken seriously.

But aside from the risk that technology exposes, there are a whole range of positives that it provides in the 21st-century classroom; post-Covid-19 when the world of education went remote, we can see the benefits it holds to both teachers and students alike when accessed safely and appropriately.

Consider some of these benefits, and how they can support disadvantaged pupils too and reflect on how this is embedded in your own classroom or provision.

Technology brings learning to life:

- Makes learning more fun and engaging;
- Encourages greater effort from students over time;

- Helps make challenging or boring subjects more interesting;
- Supports understanding of complex concepts.

Technology prepares students for the digital world:

- Develops essential 21st-century skills;
- Prepares students for digitally focused careers;
- Encourages problem-solving and collaboration;
- Helps students adapt to future challenges in education and work.

Technology can personalise learning and takes students out of the classroom:

- Supports different learning styles and abilities;
- Allows students to learn at their own pace;
- Enables teachers to tailor lessons to individual needs;
- Builds confidence and supports student success;
- Enables 'field trips' to museums, galleries and locations around the world.

Technology connects with students when they are not together:

- Aligns teaching methods with students' everyday experiences;
- Could offer AI tutors by 2027;
- Moves towards interactive learning at home and in school;
- Uses tools like Smartboards and laptops to enhance engagement;
- Remote learning allows students to access learning at home;
- Technology allows children to attend flexi schooling and online school to meet their mental and physical health needs.

Technology increases access to information when safely accessed:

- Provides easy access to a wide range of resources for teachers and students;
- Encourages self-directed learning through online platforms such as Google Classroom, Bedrock and MathsWatch;
- Allows teachers to use multimedia to support diverse learners;
- Enhances visual and interactive support to students with SEND including the use of widgets, AAC for hearing aid radio aids;
- Enhances overall learning experiences in a multi-sensory way.

Technology boosts collaboration:

- Supports real-time collaboration through digital platforms such as Kahoot;
- Encourages sharing ideas and peer feedback in a less confrontational way;
- Helps less confident students participate more comfortably;
- Allows students to interact with others who are not physically in the school building;
- Builds interpersonal and technical skills.

Technology helps students connect with the wider world:

- Enables global communication and collaboration;
- Exposes students to different perspectives and cultures;
- Supports global learning and the ability to 'see' the world;
- Prepares students for working in a global environment.

Balancing technology and traditional learning:

- Technology is constantly evolving and requires ongoing adaptation;
- Traditional learning methods remain important;
- Thoughtful integration of technology enhances learning outcomes.

Chapter Takeaways

Reflections

- To thrive in an uncertain and rapidly changing world, young people need a broad mix of transferable skills, including: critical and creative thinking, problem-solving, communication, collaboration, planning, digital literacy and resilience.
- Early intervention is key, as skills gaps in the early years often predict future outcomes. Schools must adopt a holistic, 'cradle to grave' approach that integrates cognitive, social-emotional, technical and practical skills across the curriculum, while ensuring equity by 'poverty-proofing' opportunities.
- Emerging technologies such as AI require students to develop ethical, reflective and adaptive capabilities. By fostering a growth mindset, resilience and lifelong learning, education can equip all students to navigate future challenges and succeed in both work and life.
- Children do not start school at the same point. It is not a level playing field - think of an athletic track and some children have a head start. From a young age, the children who start further along the track are having their skills topped up with every opportunity they experience. All the statistics show that this same correlation is then applied to future job prospects. To help *all* children succeed in life, schools need to be equipping their students with the skills needed for their future. We need to adopt a 'cradle to grave' approach to embed opportunities to practice, learn and use the skills children and young people need to thrive in life.

Enhanced Provision and Ideas to Support Learning

- Hands-on experiences and real-life application of knowledge in all learning.
- Use drama and role play as a stimulus across all curriculum areas.

- Team financial education.
- Teach confidence and interview skills.
- Teach that it is ok to make mistakes and how they are learning opportunities at all stages of education.
- Ensure financial education is part of the curriculum in all schools.

AI resources to support professional development

- Department for Education: https://www.gov.uk/government/collections/using-ai-in-education-settings-support-materials
- https://teachingwithchatgpt.org.uk/
- Oak Academy: https://www.thenational.academy/ai

Further Reading

- *When the adult changes everything changes* - Paul Dix
- *Life skills for youths* - Joan Dejaeghere
- *The skillful teacher* -Stephen Brookfield
- *Life skills for all learners: How to teach, assess, and report* - Amir and Guskey
- *Inside the black box* - Dylan Williams
- *Case studies showcase* - Skills Builder Partnership

Bibliography

Akpan, B. and Kennedy, T.J. eds. (2020). *Science education in theory and practice: An introductory guide to learning theory*. New York: Springer International Publishing.

Anon. (2023). 'Attendance and reading key barriers to disadvantaged pupils' progress . . .' [Online] https://educationendowmentfoundation.org.uk/news/attendance-and-reading-key-barriers-to-disadvantaged-pupils-progress-say-three-in-four-schools.

Anon. (2025). 'Financial inclusion strategy'. [Online] https://www.gov.uk/government/publications/financial-inclusion-strategy/financial-inclusion-strategy.

Anon. (2025). 'Skills England sector evidence on the growth and skills offer'. [Online] https://assets.publishing.service.gov.uk/media/6863f18b3464d9c0ad609ddf/Skills_England_-_sector_evidence_on_the_growth_and_skills_offer.pdf.

Anon. (n.d.). 'Mental Health Statistics UK | Young People'. [Online] https://www.youngminds.org.uk/about-us/media-centre/mental-health-statistics/.

Baddeley, A.D. and Hitch, G.J. (1974). *Working memory*. In G.H. Bower (ed.), *The psychology of learning and motivation: advances in research and theory*, Vol. 8. New York: Academic Press, pp. 47–89.

Ben-Shlomo, Y. and Kuh, D. (2002). 'A life course approach to chronic disease epidemiology: Conceptual models, empirical challenges and interdisciplinary perspectives'. *International Journal of Epidemiology*, 31(2), 285–293.

Bocock, L., del Pozo Segura, J.M. and Hillary, J. (2025) *Building foundations: The implications of research on childhood skill development for addressing future skills needs in England*. Slough: National Foundation for Educational Research (NFER). https://www.nfer.ac.uk/publications/the-skills-imperative-2035-the-implications-of-research-on-childhood-skill-development-for-addressing-future-skills-needs-in-england/.

Bocock, L., Scott, M. and Hillary, J. (2025). *Skills Imperative 2035: Creating a system of lifelong learning to provide the essential skills for tomorrow's workforce.* [Online] https://www.nfer.ac.uk/publications/skills-imperative-2035-final-report/.

Bronfenbrenner, U. (1986). Ecology of the family as a context for human development: Research perspectives. *Developmental Psychology*, 22(6), 723–742. https://doi.org/10.1037/0012-1649.22.6.723.

Bryce, T. and Brown, E. (2023). 'Ausubel's meaningful learning re-visited'. *Current* Psychology, 43(5), 4579-4598.

Cattan, S., Fitzsimons, E., Goodman, A., Phimister, A. and Ploubidis, G.B. (2022) *The early years: foundations for life, health and learning.* London: Institute for Fiscal Studies.

Department for Education (DfE). (2021). *Skills for jobs: Lifelong learning for opportunity and growth.* London: Department for Education. https://www.gov.uk/government/publications/skills-for-jobs-lifelong-learning-for-opportunity-and-growth.

Department for Education. (2025). 'No child left behind in plans to narrow the digital divide in education'. [Online] https://www.gov.uk/government/news/no-child-left-behind-in-plans-to-narrow-the-digital-divide-in-education.

Department for Education. (2025). 'Research and analysis executive summary with introduction and next steps'. [Online] https://www.gov.uk/government/publications/ai-skills-for-the-uk-workforce/executive-summary-with-introduction-and-next-steps.

Donnelly, M., McLanahan, S., Brooks-Gunn, J., Garfinkel, I., Wagner, B.G. and Jacobsen, W.C. (2019) *Extra-curricular activities, soft skills and social mobility.* London: Social Mobility Commission.

Dweck, C.S. (1999). *Self-theories: Their role in motivation, personality, and development.* Philadelphia, PA: Psychology Press.

Education Policy Institute. (2024). Annual report 2024: Foreword & executive summary. [Online] https://epi.org.uk/annual-report-2024-foreword-executive-summary/?utm_source=chatgpt.com.

Elder, G. (1998). 'The life course as developmental theory'. *Child Development*, 69(1), 1–12.

Fernstein, L. (2003). 'Inequality in the early cognitive development of British children in the early 1970 cohort'. *Economica*, 70(277), 73–97.

Galinksy, E. (2010). *Mind in the making: The seven essential life skills every child needs.* Glasgow: Harper Collins.

GOV.UK, 2026. *Gov.UK.* [Online] https://www.gov.uk/government/news/450000-disadvantaged-pupils-could-benefit-from-ai-tutoring-tool.

Heckman, J. (2000). 'Policies to foster human capital'. *Research in Economics*, 54(1), 3–56.

IFF Research. (2023). *Employer Skills Survey 2022: UK Report.* London: Department for Education. https://www.gov.uk/government/publications/employer-skills-survey-2022-uk-report.

Ofsted. (2024). *Strong foundations in the first years of school.* Manchester: Office for Standards in Education, Children's Services and Skills. https://www.gov.uk/government/publications/strong-foundations-in-the-first-years-of-school.

Money and Pensions Service. (2025). *Measuring financial literacy of children aged four to six years.* London: Money and Pensions Service. https://maps.org.uk/en/publications/research/2024/measuring-financial-literacy-children-aged-four-to-six.

Peck, D. (2025). '10 Top online learning trends for 2025: Definitive guide'. [Online] https://www.devlinpeck.com/content/online-learning-trends.

Robinson, D. (2024). *Access to extra-curricular provision and the association with outcomes.* London: Education Policy Institute. https://epi.org.uk/publications-and-research/access-to-extra-curricular-provision-and-the-association-with-outcomes.

Shay, D., Shavit, Y. and Sasson, I. (2025). 'Beyond the cradle: Effects of family income in the first 1,000 days on educational achievement later in life'. *European Sociological Review*, 42(2), 218–236.

Skills Builder Partnership. (2026). *Skills Builder Global.* https://www.skillsbuilder.org.

The London Foundation for Banking and Finance. (2025). *The London Foundation for Banking and Finance.* [Online] https://www.lfbf.org.uk/financial-capability-lfbf-calls-for-a-bold-shift-to-grasp-a-once-in-a-generation-opportunity.

Willingham, D.T. (2009). *Why don't students like school? A cognitive scientist answers questions about how the mind works and what it means for the classroom.* San Francisco, CA: Jossey-Bass.

Willingham, D. (2017). 'A mental model of the learner: Teaching the basic science of educational psychology to future teachers'. *International Mind, Brain, and Education Society*, 11(4), 166–175.

Willingham, D. (n.d.). *Simple memory model.* [Online] https://www.ollielovell.com/ollie-lovell-oliver-lovlel-josh-goodrich-steplab-instructional-coaching-diagnosis-daniel-willingham-simple-model-of-memory/.

Yanatma, S. (2025). 'GenAI job postings rise across Europe: Which countries lead the way?' *Euronews.* https://www.euronews.com/business/2025/06/29/genai-job-postings-rise-across-europe-which-countries-lead-the-way.

Young Enterprise. (2025). *Making the classroom count: The role of financial education in schools.* London: Young Enterprise.

YoungMinds. (2025). *Mental health statistics UK: Young people*. London: YoungMinds. https://www.youngminds.org.uk/about-us/media-centre/mental-health-statistics.

7

Vocabulary Development for All

Vocabulary development has a huge impact on a child's development and future prospects. Having a well-rounded vocabulary enhances communication skills, enables people to articulate feelings, therefore improving wellbeing and building self-esteem. Vocabulary is not just about spoken language, it is about the way in which we communicate effectively which is an essential life skill.

Pre-reading Reflection Questions

- How is oracy embedded across all areas of the curriculum in your school or setting, rather than being treated as an additional or isolated skill?
- What evidence do we use to track meaningful vocabulary progression over time, and how do we challenge ourselves to ensure all children – particularly the most vulnerable – are closing the language gap rather than maintaining it?

Vocabulary – What Does This Mean?

Let's start this chapter by considering what we mean by vocabulary. Quite simply, vocabulary is the collection of words that an individual person knows, which, in the case of a child, is hugely influenced by their early childhood experiences. This early childhood vocabulary can be categorised into two groups:

- Passive vocabulary: the collection of words that a person understands but does not actively use in their day-to-day communications and interactions.
- Active vocabulary: describes the words that a person uses in their day-to-day communication (this includes both spoken and written communication).

When we consider applying this in terms of children, a young child will have a range of words in their active vocabulary that they use in their day-to-day life. For example, run, climb, play, toilet or snack. However, they most likely have a wider vocabulary too which

DOI: 10.4324/9781003624004-7

includes words, such as delicate or frustrated, which they passively understand but they are not at the developmental stage of using as part of their active vocabulary.

When we consider vocabulary development in children it is essential that we understand that the earlier it is acquired, the better a child's life chances. Research carried out by Hart and Risley document this in the '30-million-word gap' – their research shows that children from low-income backgrounds hear, on average, 30 million words less than their more advantaged peers by the age of four (Hart and Risley, 1995).

Vocabulary is essential for effective communication and for children this begins with oral communication before progressing onto written communication. We know that children who have a broad range of vocabulary are likely to have a deeper understanding of the world as their vocabulary allows for more nuanced and precise expressions in their conversation; allowing them to challenge ideas, reflect on experiences and share their knowledge in more detail. It is also important to understand that there is a direct correlation between a wide range of vocabulary in children and a higher level of reading comprehension as they progress through their education. Let us take the 2017 SATs paper as an example of this. The reading paper included an article about the English Channel. If a child does not understand that the English Channel is a body of water, then this whole article will not make sense, and will subsequently limit their comprehension of much of the text.

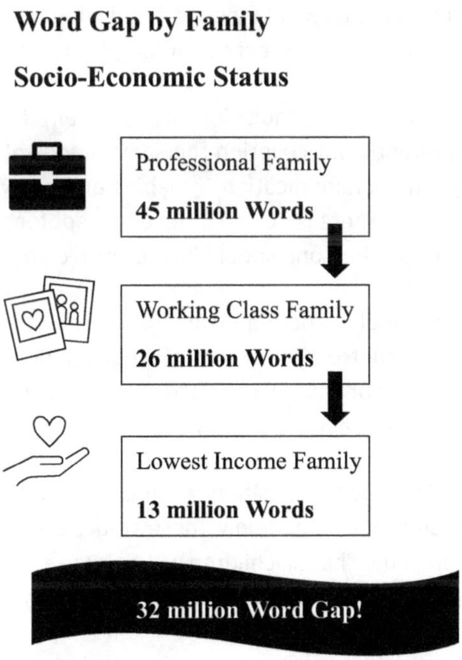

Figure 7.1 The 30-million-word gap

(TICK Hub, adapted from Hart and Risely, 1995)

You can find the article excerpt here: https://www.sats-papers.co.uk/sats-papers/ks2/english/2017/ks2-english-2017-reading-booklet.pdf

When we consider how vocabulary is learned there are three main ways:

- Direct experiences – where children learn new vocabulary through real life experiences and situations.
- Educational experiences – where children are explicitly taught vocabulary through their school curricula.
- Reading – exposure to high-quality texts, listening to stories and, later, reading independently gives children exposure to a wide range of language which expands their active and passive vocabulary.

Interestingly, in his 1921 work, Ludwig Wittgenstein, a leading 20th-century philosopher of language, proposed that: 'The limit of my language means the limits of my world' (Wittgenstein, 1921). His concern was that we are limited by what we can say and think, and that this is limited by the languages that we can express ourselves. Alarmingly, over 100 years later not only does this appear to ring true for many secondary school-age children, but secondary school teachers are telling us that the word gap is getting wider, with worryingly significant consequences (The Oxford Language Report, 2018).

Ages and Stages of Language Acquisition

Let's now look at the ages and stages of language acquisition and the effects that this has on children's development, which also affects their long-term development.

In the UK, the stages of language acquisition are generally broken down into several phases, often defined differently but covering the same stages of language development. This starts with prelinguistic communication in babies and evolves over time into more complete sentence structures. There is no linear development for speech and language but there are signs to be aware of when one should be concerned about development.

Language development is complex and highly individual as it is impacted by a number of factors outside of the child's control. The stages of language development include babble, the single word stage, the two word stage, the telegraphic stage (focusing on short, concise phrases of 2–5 words) and eventually the multi-word stage.

At the earliest stages of language acquisition, even before babies talk and truly babble, there are signs of language acquisition. Below, these stages are broken down by age, however it is important to remember that all children will develop speech at different rates and that there are a number of factors, beyond human control, that will also impact this guide:

- **By 6 months old**, most babies respond to sounds by turning their head, may be startled by loud noises, and enjoy watching faces and making eye contact. They recognise familiar voices and often become excited when they hear a caregiver approaching. Babies at this age smile and laugh in response to others, make sounds such as cooing and babbling, and use different cries for different needs. They also begin to make noises back when spoken to, showing early turn-taking.

- **By one year old**, babies listen more carefully and can turn toward someone speaking across the room. They recognise their name, enjoy action songs and rhymes, and begin to understand familiar words like 'bye-bye' or 'up', especially when actions are used. They babble strings of sounds, point or make noises to gain attention, and enjoy simple games such as peekaboo. Many will say one or two recognisable words and enjoy taking turns in simple 'conversations'.
- **By around 18 months old**, children enjoy music, singing and looking at simple picture books with adults. They understand many more words than they can say and can follow simple instructions or questions. They may say up to 20 single words, use lots of babble while playing and copy adults' words and actions. Pretend play begins to emerge, and children use pointing, actions or words to get attention while becoming gradually more independent.
- **By two years old**, children can focus on activities for longer and enjoy listening to simple stories. They understand hundreds of words and can follow simple questions and instructions. Vocabulary grows to around 50 words or more, and children begin combining two or three words into short sentences. They enjoy pretend play, explore more independently, copy sounds and words frequently and may become frustrated when they are not understood.
- **By three years old**, children understand simple stories, longer instructions and basic 'who', 'what' and 'where' questions. They use short sentences of four to five words, ask many questions, and begin using grammar such as plurals. Speech becomes clearer, although some sounds are still tricky. Children show interest in playing with others, talk about their likes and dislikes and may briefly stammer as their language develops.
- **By four years old, the average age of children starting primary education in England**, children understand more complex ideas such as colour, number, time and simple reasons why things happen. They use longer sentences, link ideas with words like 'and' and talk about past and future events. They enjoy cooperative and imaginative play, tell short stories, start conversations and use words to solve conflicts. Speech is mostly clear to unfamiliar listeners, with only a few difficult sounds remaining.
- **By five years old, the end of the foundation stage**, children can follow longer instructions while continuing an activity and understand stories without pictures. They take turns in longer conversations, stay on topic and use detailed sentences to explain ideas. They understand positional and sequencing words like 'first', 'next' and 'between', talk confidently about real and imagined events, and are understood clearly by others most of the time.
- **By seven years old, the beginning of key stage 2 education**, children can concentrate for longer periods and remember stories told over time. They understand that words can have multiple meanings and that different words can mean the same thing. Language is used to explain ideas, solve problems, tell jokes and give reasons.

Sentences are longer and more complex, conversations flow smoothly and speech is clear to unfamiliar listeners.

- **By 11 years old, the end of primary education**, children use language to link ideas, make predictions and draw conclusions. They tell detailed and imaginative stories, understand different points of view and explain their reasoning clearly. Vocabulary becomes more advanced, conversations can be sustained with a wide range of people and spoken language is fluent and clear.
- **By 14 years**, young people use longer, more complex sentences and a wide range of joining words to explain abstract ideas. They understand sarcasm, idioms, humour and can shift topics easily in conversation. Language style changes depending on the audience, and slang may be used appropriately with peers while more formal language is used with adults.
- **By 17 years**, young people can follow very complex instructions, recognise when they do not understand something and ask for clarification. They can switch confidently between informal and formal language and tell long, detailed stories with clear structure.
- **By 18 years**, young people can use language flexibly and precisely across situations. They understand and follow complex directions, use persuasive arguments and explain misunderstandings clearly. Vocabulary is broad, sentence structure is advanced and stories are well organised. They move smoothly between topics, fully understand sarcasm and adjust their language easily depending on audience and context.

Background and Barriers

Of course, young people's language development varies considerably, with some learners progressing more quickly than others. Various factors may contribute to barriers in language development. Examining these underlying influences allows us to better understand how such barriers arise and how they can be effectively addressed and reduced.

A substantial body of research highlights the critical importance of early language acquisition (Hart and Risley, 1995, Bercow, 2008, Bercow, Fricke and Hughes, 2018, Shonkoff and Philips, 2000, Snow, Burns and Griffin, 1998). This is not a new concept within 21st-century education; rather, the significance of speech and language development has been recognised for well over a century. As early as the late nineteenth and early twentieth centuries, researchers were exploring the role of language in cognitive development. John Thelwall (1806), often regarded as the first British speech and language pathologist, made notable contributions through his work on speech disorders and their cognitive implications. Later, in the 1960s, Dorothea McCarthy further advanced understanding of language acquisition, an area that remains a key focus of contemporary research. Evidence consistently demonstrates that children's language abilities in the early years are a strong predictor of their learning and academic progress throughout their schooling.

Case Study: The Bishops C of E and RC Primary School, Chelmsford

Liz Lee, Senior Leader

I have seen the vital importance of creating a rich vocabulary environment. High-quality vocabulary development isn't just a feature of early learning, it is the foundation of it. It's something that must be woven into everyday life and practice.

Throughout my career, I have encountered a wide range of communication needs. However, in the years following the Covid-19 lockdowns, I have observed a noticeable shift. More children seem to struggle with vocabulary naming and usage and there has been a marked increase in signs of anxiety, including selective mutism. Many young children now appear more hesitant to express themselves, struggling to link words to objects or to communicate their wants and needs effectively.

In response, many settings have implemented targeted strategies: small group work, specialist toolkits, tailored interventions and government-led initiatives. These approaches are undoubtedly valuable and have their place in a comprehensive support plan.

However, I often return to a simple but powerful piece of advice given to me when I was a newly qualified teacher. A wise colleague once said: 'Strategies and interventions are useful, but the most powerful tool you have is the connection you make.'

Case Study: The Bishops C of E and RC Primary School, Chelmsford

This was highlighted to me during a pre-school transition meeting. I met a child and the preschool staff explained that this child had been in their provision for two years and during that time, had not spoken a single word, not to adults, not to peers. Making no attempt to communicate using spoken language. Although, moved happily within the setting, exploring the different areas and liked being alongside other children.

When I spoke to the parents, they described a child who was talkative at home, confident in her communication and fluent in another language aside from English. At home, she made her needs known with ease and clarity. It quickly became clear that the child was showing signs of selective mutism within the nursery setting.

The staff were doing their best, and they shared the various strategies they had been using to support her.

At the transition visit, I introduced myself gently to the child. I returned several more times before the new school year began, always giving her a wave and a calm, quiet hello, nothing too intrusive, just a familiar face. I was conscious of wanting to be present without being overwhelming.

In September, the child joined my class of 30 children, along with my Learning Support Assistant. During the initial settling-in period, I focused on parallel play, non-verbal interactions and shared silent moments of connection. Then, one day seemingly out of nowhere I heard an answer while doing the register, in the smallest voice.

Inside, I was quietly jumping for joy.

From that moment, the spoken language gradually became more frequent; at first, mainly directed toward me. Then spontaneous language during play, particularly when interacting with me in a small group.

Then Christmas arrived, bringing with it the excitement of nativity rehearsals. Something changed. It was as if the 'pillars' of her anxiety had crumbled. Suddenly, she was speaking freely, not just with me, but with her peers, with other adults and across all contexts. Her speech was rapid, expressive, joyful. Friendships blossomed and social and emotional development took a huge leap forward.

It wasn't just strategies or interventions. It was time, patience, safety and connection. It sounds simple but meaningful connections for a child who is struggling to express themselves is everything.

Case study question: How intentionally do we prioritise time, emotional safety and authentic connection - alongside formal strategies - to unlock children's confidence to communicate?

As educational professionals, we recognise that effective communication skills are fundamental to children's development across all areas of the curriculum. A broad and active vocabulary enables children to clearly express their needs, wishes and emotions, supporting the development of positive relationships with peers, families and the adults who care for them. In turn, strong communication skills help children to form healthy connections with the wider world and the environment around them. In 2025, 79.5% of children achieved the Good Level of Development for Communication and Language. This means that 20% of children leaving the EYFS were not at the expected level for their age for communication skills and language acquisition (Department for Education, 2025).

In practice, this means that in a class of 30 pupils, six of these children will not have the language and communication skills to effectively communicate as they move into Year 1. Research shows that if a child attends an early years setting the quality of their education that they receive significantly impacts their development (Sylva, 2014).

Early development during a child's first five years can have a lasting influence on future achievement (OECD, 2020). This impact extends beyond primary education to secondary schooling and life beyond formal education. Over the long term, early developmental experiences can affect an individual's wellbeing, socio-economic outcomes, mental and physical health and overall resilience (OECD, 2020).

Therefore, this early input into language development in homes and settings is crucial for supporting children's life changes. In 2022, OFSTED reported that:

> A high-quality early years education is vitally important. Children attend early years provision at a crucial developmental point in their lives. The education and care that they receive affects not only future educational attainment but also their future health and happiness.

Breaking Down and Raising Barriers

In the next part of this chapter we will be looking more closely at the barriers that children face in their development of language and their acquisition of vocabulary before exploring what we can do in schools, early years settings and when working with families to break down these barriers.

First, let's explore the social economic barriers that could affect a child's ability to acquire, explore and retain vocabulary. A family's socio-economic status is a known predictor of parents' language input and children's language development (Schwab and Williams, 2016).

Research shows that children who come from families with a lower socio-economic status are more likely to receive less high-quality language input at home and have less high-quality language-based experiences in their formative years Hart and Risley (1995). This could include sharing less stories and having less experiences where language-rich conversation is taking place. The lack of these experiences puts these children at an early disadvantage compared to their more language-rich peers. When considering socio-economic factors, we must also be aware of the impact of financial constraints on resources, experiences and education at a young age. Children who are being raised in poverty may not have access to the same experiences, resources and *time* that their more affluent peers have.

The National Literacy Trust (2024) found that one in eight children under 18 did not own a book; and that book ownership was lower in disadvantaged children. This was linked, at the time, to the 'cost of living crisis' and the impact this has on book purchases (National Literacy Trust, 2024).

Programmes, such as the Letterbox club (The Book Trust), are aiming to tackle this in schools and support book ownership and promote a love of reading and therefore language. They set out their intentions for their work, stating their ambitions to make reading a daily part of life for every child due to the profound effect on overcoming disadvantage (Book Trust, 2025).

In the same way, in some areas of the country, children from low-income families are less likely to access high-quality pre-school education and will almost certainly have less opportunities to be read to. The impact of parental education is also a hinging factor in language development. If a child has a family with poor vocabulary language and experiences then the language they hear at home will be significantly less than peers from a language-rich background.

There has been research carried out into this. In the 1990s, Hart and Risley highlighted the '30-million-word gap' (Hart and Risley, 1995). The research found a significant disparity between the language experiences of children from affluent and lower-income backgrounds. To obtain these results, they recorded the language spoken and heard in the homes of three-year-old children. Hart and Risley found that a child in a family receiving benefits heard 30 million words less than a child growing up in a professional family. Ultimately, this research concluded that children in more affluent families are exposed to far more language in their early years, leading to a larger repertoire of vocabulary and stronger language skills by the time they start school. This all highlights the crucial importance of language interventions for children before they even start school – an intervention which is surely worth funding and effort?

Families that are deemed language poor are less likely to expose children to rich texts, songs, rhymes or conversations and general discussions. The recordings from the research carried out by Hart and Risley (1995) also showed that children in poorer families spoke around four times fewer new words per day.

Similarly, Weisleder and Fernald (2013) explored this further and found that as well as the language a child says, there are dramatic differences in the number of words children in different social economic groups understand. This difference is even present by the time children are 18 months old. Children's language at age five is the single most important factor in predicting literacy at age 11 – it is more important, they claim, than behaviour, peer relationships, emotional wellbeing, positive interaction and attention (Weisleder and Fernald, 2013).

Case Study: Burnham on Crouch Primary School, Essex

Louise Boroughs - Deputy Head teacher

Embedding Vocabulary-Rich Practice to Remove Barriers to Learning

At our school, the biggest barrier to learning for many pupils – particularly those who are disadvantaged – lies in limited vocabulary and underlying speech and language needs. A high proportion of children enter the Early Years Foundation Stage (EYFS) with communication skills significantly below age-related expectations. This reality has shaped a whole-school commitment to building a vocabulary-rich curriculum that prioritises language development as the foundation for equity, access and long-term academic success.

Our vocabulary strategy begins in EYFS through consistent, immersive practices. Drawing Club, for example, provides a playful yet structured daily opportunity for children to hear and use rich, ambitious vocabulary in meaningful contexts. Through stories, shared drawings and imaginative prompts, practitioners model expressive language while encouraging children to orally rehearse new words in their own narratives. Poetry Baskets further strengthen this foundation, allowing pupils to internalise rhyme, rhythm and prosody. Regular repetition of high-quality poems builds language patterns, supports memory and exposes children to sophisticated vocabulary long before they may be able to decode it independently.

A central component of our approach is Helicopter Stories, which ensures every child is both a storyteller and a valued contributor to a shared narrative space. This approach has been particularly impactful for pupils with speech, language and communication needs, as it creates a low-pressure, high-engagement environment where adults can skilfully scaffold oral storytelling. By scribing children's words verbatim and bringing their ideas to life through performance, we reinforce the message that every voice matters – an essential principle in an inclusive, equitable setting.

These practices sit within a carefully designed curriculum built around high-quality texts. Across the school, units begin with rich, diverse literature selected not only for its narrative quality but for its linguistic depth.

Texts are chosen to introduce ambitious vocabulary, expand pupils' cultural capital and expose them to varied language structures. Explicit vocabulary instruction is woven

Figure 7.2 Example of poetry basket resources used in Reception to promote vocabulary, communication and early literacy skills

throughout lessons, supported by strong oracy expectations and consistent visual scaffolds.

The impact is clear: pupils who begin their school journey with limited language leave EYFS increasingly confident in articulating ideas, using newly acquired vocabulary with accuracy and pride. As they move through school, this strong early foundation enables them to engage more deeply with reading, writing and wider curriculum learning.

Figure 7.3 Example of a classroom washing line used to display key vocabulary, prompts and learning resources throughout a sequence of lessons

Our approach demonstrates that vocabulary development is not an add-on but a core equity strategy. By intentionally immersing children in language-rich experiences from their very first days in school, we ensure that every learner – regardless of starting point – has the linguistic tools to thrive.

Alongside this, family diversity also has an environmental influence on children's early language experiences, including how different households value books and nursery rhymes and make opportunities for talk and discussions. In an increasingly technology-driven generation, fewer children may regularly experience activities such as bedtime stories or singing rhymes during everyday routines. It is therefore essential that families are supported to engage in meaningful interactions that promote vocabulary development at home, as well as within early years settings.

Government figures show that, in England, around 25% of children start schools with poorly developed speech and language skills. Speech and language are identified as the most common type of special education need in English primary schools and the second most common need identified in Education, Health, Care Plans (EHCP) (Long and Roberts, 2025). Crucially, Law (2017) found that: 'Children with language difficulties at age five were four times more likely to have reading difficulties in adulthood, three times as likely to have mental health problems, and twice as likely to be unemployed when they reached adulthood.'

The benefits of vocabulary acquisition do not stop at any stage of education, in fact, the importance of language acquisition progresses throughout adult life in the workplace as well. Secondary schools report the impact of language and vocabulary on progress and attainment of older children, with as much significance as it has in primary education. In 2018, Oxford University Press cited that 60% of secondary teachers surveyed (of the 840 secondary teachers who took part) reported that the number of students who have a limited vocabulary is either increasing or significantly increasing (The Oxford Language Report, 2018). Further still, 80% of the secondary teachers reported that students who have a limited vocabulary find reading national test papers challenging and felt that those children achieved worse results in national tests (The Oxford Language Report, 2018). Eighty percent of secondary teachers surveyed reflected that in their school, the word/vocabulary gap leads to lower self-esteem in pupils, and this has a negative impact on behaviour further with these students being identified as those who are less likely to stay on in education. The significance of this is shocking. The report found that 66% of pupils who are at risk of permanent exclusion from a mainstream secondary school have language difficulties and 81% of children with formally identified emotional and behavioural disorders have significantly below average language abilities (Grove, 2023).

Aside from these needs there are a small number of children who have specific difficulties acquiring language and vocabulary. This could be due to English being an additional language, difficulties with attention and listening skills or specific speech and language difficulties. Indeed, it's clear that if children do not get the chance to acquire vocabulary rapidly and apply it in a range of situations that they will fall further behind rather than catch up with age. So, let's now look at how schools can support language and vocabulary; reducing barriers for pupils and closing gaps.

Language Development/Oracy

We know that disadvantaged children know less words. There has been lots written about the importance of both oracy and vocabulary development. The benefits of explicitly teaching vocabulary, particularly for disadvantaged pupils, are well established. To have a repertoire of vocabulary to draw upon helps not only comprehension but aids fluency, supports writing and enables all to contribute to a discussion and articulate their thoughts and feelings. Knowing more words helps to build confidence with their communication skills. Research suggests that children need to know 95% of words within a book for comfortable comprehension (Quigley, 2016).

For children to develop their language they need to have enough exposure to it multiple times. Without this exposure we run the risk of a word gap amongst our young people. Most children need to meet, use and spell new words repeatedly for the words to embed into their long-term memory. Improving vocabulary will also improve reading ability. There have been studies carried out which revealed that children who were better communicators were also more resilient, which of course is a key skill needed for life (Werner and Smith, 1992).

There are a number of ways in which vocabulary can be taught in schools:

1. Introduce words daily. Explain what the words means and provide examples of how the word can be used. Collect these words and display them clearly for the children to see.
2. Teach new words to the class with an accompanying picture. Provide contexts in which the word can be used.

Recently, there have been updates about what the new curriculum will look like (GOV.UK, 2025). A new addition to the National Curriculum will be an Oracy Framework. This framework, based on speaking, listening and communication, aims to provide a structured progression for schools to follow to help prepare children and young people of this vital life skill. Voice 21, an oracy charity, have campaigned for oracy to have more of a prominent status in the education system.

The term 'oracy' was coined by Wilkinson in the 1960s to emphasise the educational importance of spoken language skills, on a par with reading and writing skills; he defined oracy as 'the ability to use the oral skills of speaking and listening'. The concept was championed in the UK by the National Oracy Project in the late 1980s but was abandoned when government priorities became focused on reading, writing and mathematics. Now, the term is being used more widely, reflecting a growing awareness of the educational and social importance of spoken language skills. Two key reasons for a focus on oracy education are its impact on:

- Children's cognitive development and learning in school; and
- Children's preparation for participation in the wider world.

Children are not born with language 'hard-wired' into their cognition. Voice 21 believes that 'Oracy skills are vital to success in school and in life. And yet, for many children, especially those growing up in poverty, opportunities to develop these vital skills are missed' (Voice 21, 2024).

In the same way, the Oracy Education Commission's report 'We need to talk' (2024) (Oracy Education Commission) highlighted the urgent need for schools to prioritise oracy in the curriculum for both primary and secondary skills to address inequalities and improve student outcomes. Research carried out by Sedova, Sedlacek and Svaricek (2019) revealed that there is a compelling link between the amount of time students spend talking about the content of their learning and the attainment and progress they then make.

How Can Oracy Be Taught Effectively in Schools?

- Think about the opportunities you provide for students to articulate their thoughts. By allowing students time to talk about what they are thinking improves their communication skills and goes some way to deepen their thinking.

- Use 'Think Pair Share' to allow students to discuss what they are learning. The children can orally prepare their answer. Bring their learning and connections they have and speak about this.
- In the same way, schools will need to teach young people how to actively listen. Children will need to be taught what listening actually means. How to listen with feelings, listen in a caring way and listening in a way to learn something new.
- Scaffold pupils' talk:

Strategies for Talk	*Description*
Sentence stems	Provide examples of speaking structures around the classroom. These provide a lead in for children: First, At the beginning, In my opinion, Following on from what . . . Said . . . I believe, in my opinion . . . I wonder if, I don't believe
Think Pair Share	This gives students the opportunity to explore their thinking before speaking in a big group.
A word or phrase a day	Place a word by the door. As the students enter or leave the classroom, they have to say the word out loud.
Talk roles	In pairs or a group assign specific roles to students. 1. Instigator – will start the discussion 2. Prober – asks for more detail 3. Challenger – puts forward another view point or a different opinion 4. Clarifyer – sums up the discussion

The new Oracy Framework which is being introduced into the new National Curriculum will provide a structure for all schools to address this crucial skill needed for the modern world. The intention is to bridge the gap between the language children encounter in school, the language they hear at home, and the language they will need and use in the world of work. There is also something to be said about the use of oracy to help smooth the transition for students as they move from primary to secondary school.

Moving into secondary education is a significant transition. Pupils face not only a wider range of subjects and increasingly complex content, but also the social and emotional challenges of settling into a new school environment. As the curriculum becomes more demanding, they encounter higher-level vocabulary that may be unfamiliar. Deignan, Candarli, and Oxley (2022) note that as students progress from primary to secondary, the language of school moves even further away from the language of home. A carefully designed oracy education can ease this transition, offering vital support – particularly for the most disadvantaged students.

- Consider the manipulatives and scaffolds used for students especially in Year 7 and Year 8. There seems to be a big difference between what is available for children in Year 6 and Year 7 with many of the scaffolds being removed in the first year of secondary school.
- Manipulatives should be removed when the knowledge has improved – this is not linked to age.

Chapter Takeaways

Reflections

- Early language acquisition impacts life chances for children.
- Early language does not happen by chance, it needs to be planned and explicitly taught.
- Language acquisition and vocabulary is impacted by reading, life experiences and socio-economic factors.

Now Consider

- How is oracy at the heart of all teaching and learning?
- How is language accessed by children in all vulnerable groups as well as the universal offer?
- How is reading promoted in all ages, particularly for those who are more reluctant readers by characteristics?
- What does language and vocabulary progress look like in your school or setting and how is this challenged?

Enhanced Provision and Ideas to Support Learning

- The Poetry Basket and Helicopter stories.
- NELI speech and language programmes.
- ELKLAN speech, language and communication.
- The use of visual prompts and aids in classrooms.
- How are children supported in their individual needs?
- Consider the role of parent workshops and play and stay sessions.

- Bedtime story hours in schools.
- Bedtime book sacks to go home at weekends to promote sharing of books.
- Vocabulary jars in classrooms.
- Language-rich schools with all adults promoting high levels of oracy.

Further Reading

- *The 30 million word gap* – Hart and Risley
- *Why closing the word gap matters: The Oxford Language Report* – Oxford University Press
- *The confident teacher* – Alex Quigley
- *How to explain absolutely everything to absolutely everyone* – Andy Tharby
- *Disciplinary literacy* – Shareen Wilkinson
- *The reading gap* – Alex Quigley

Bibliography

Bercow, J. (2008). *The Bercow Report: A review of services for children and young people (0–19) with speech, language and communication needs.* Nottingham: Department for Children, Schools and Families.

Bercow, J., Fricke, S. and Hughes, N. (2018). *Bercow: Ten years on – an independent review of provision for children and young people with speech, language and communication needs in England.* London: I CAN and the Royal College of Speech and Language Therapists.

Clark, C. (2024). *Children and Young People's Reading in 2024.* London: National Literacy Trust. https://literacytrust.org.uk/research-services/research-reports/children-and-young-peoples-reading-in-2024/.

Commission on the Future of Oracy Education in England (2024) *We Need to Talk: The Report of the Commission on the Future of Oracy Education in England.* London: Voice 21 and Impetus. https://oracyeducationcommission.co.uk/oec-report/.

Deignan, A., Candarli, D. and Oxley, F. (2022). *The linguistic challenge of the transition to secondary school: A corpus study of academic language.* London:Taylor & Francis Group.

Department for Education. (2025). *Early years foundation stage profile results.* [Online] https://explore-education-statistics.service.gov.uk/find-statistics/early-years-foundation-stage-profile-results/2024-25.

GOV.UK. (2025). *Curriculum and assessment review final report.* London: Department for Education.

Grove, N., 2023. *Abstracts from RCSLT Conference 2023: Embracing the future together.* [Online] https://www.speechtherapy.co.uk/resources/PDFs/Conferences/Intl-J-Lang-Comm-Disor-2024-Abstracts-from-RCSLT-Conference-2023-Embracing-the-future-together.pdf.

Harris, S. (2025). *That Poverty Guy.* https://thatpovertyguy.substack.com/.

Hart, B. and Risley, T.R. (1995). *Meaningful differences in the everyday experience of young American children.* Baltimore: P.H. Brookes Publishing Company.

Law, D. (2017). 'Speech and language therapy interventions for children with primary speech and/or language disorders'. *Cochrane Database of Systematic Reviews,* 2017(1), 1–21. https://doi.org/10.1002/14651858.CD012490.

Long, R. and Roberts, N. (2025). *Special Educational Needs: Support in England.* House of Commons Library Research Briefing No. 07020. London: House of Commons Library. Available at: https://commonslibrary.parliament.uk/research-briefings/sn07020/.

OECD. (2020). *Early learning and child well-being: A study of five-year-olds in England, Estonia, and the United States.* Paris: OECD Publishing.

Oracy Education Commission. (2024). *We need to talk*. Oracy Education Commission. https://oracyeducationcommission.co.uk/oec-report/.

Oxford University Press. (2018). 'Why closing the word gap matters: Oxford Language Report'. [Online] https://www.naae.org.uk/wp-content/uploads/2018/06/Oxford-Word-Gap-report.pdf.

Quigley, A. (2016). *The confident teacher*. London:Routledge.

Schwab, J. and Williams, C. (2016). 'Language learning, socioeconomic status, and child-directed speech'. *Cognitive Science*, 7(4), 264–275.

Sedova, K., Sedlacek, M. and Svaricek, R. (2019). 'Student participation in dialogic teaching: Evidence from secondary school classrooms'. *Learning, Culture and Social Interaction*, 21, 195–204.

Shonkoff, J.P. and Phillips, D.A. (eds.) (2000). *From neurons to neighborhoods: The science of early childhood development*. Washington, DC: National Academy Press.

Snow, C.E., Burns, M.S. and Griffin, P. (eds.) (1998). *Preventing reading difficulties in young children*. Washington, DC: National Academy Press.

Sylva, K. (2014). 'The role of families and pre-school in educational disadvantage'. *Oxford Review of Education*, 40(6), 680–695.

The Oxford Language Report. (2018). *Why closing the word gap matters*. Oxford Language Report. https://www.oup.com.cn/test/word-gap.pdf.

Thelwall, J. (1806). *The choice speaker; or exercises on elocution*. London: Richard Phillips.

Weisleder, A. and Fernald, A. (2013). 'Talking to children matters: Early language experience strengthens processing and builds vocabulary'. *Psychological Science*, 24(11). https://doi.org/10.1177/0956797613488145.

Werner, E.E. and Smith, R.S. (1992). *Overcoming the odds: High risk children from birth to adulthood*. Ithaca, NY: Cornell University Press.

Wittgenstein, L. (1921). *Tractatus Logico-Philosophicus*. Translated by D.F. Pears and B.F. McGuinness. London: Routledge.

8

Curriculum Mapping

In every school it is essential that the curriculum is well planned; offering children the chance to develop lifelong learning skills and knowledge through a broad, balanced and aspiration curriculum.

Pre-reading Reflection Questions

- How well aligned is your curriculum and where do gaps currently exist?
- To what extent does your curriculum provide a clear and coherent learning pathway for pupils, rather than a collection of disconnected experiences?
- How do teachers' prior knowledge, experience, and self-efficacy influence how the curriculum is interpreted and enacted in classrooms?
- How effectively do our school culture, systems and leadership practices support the successful implementation and ongoing refinement of the curriculum?

Curriculum Planning

The term curriculum, translated to Latin 'currere', means racecourse (Wikipedia, 2026). If a curriculum is thought about in this way, then one might imagine a pathway, with steps along the way - imagine the racing gates as the beginning of the Early years Foundation Stage and the furlongs being the years or hurdles of education. The Department for Education describes a school curriculum as the totality of learning and other experiences in schools (Department for Education, 2014). Ultimately, this is the sum of learning experiences for young people in schools.

There are different forms of curriculum (Phaeton and Stears, 2017). The *macro level* (intended curriculum), where policy decisions and goals are set; the *meso level* (implemented curriculum), where teachers interpret and enact these intentions in schools and classrooms; and the *micro level* (attained curriculum), which reflects learners' experiences, outcomes, and

DOI: 10.4324/9781003624004-8

competencies (Phaeton and Stears, 2017). Research consistently shows that misalignment often occurs between these levels, particularly between the intended and implemented curriculum, due to factors such as selective use of curriculum documents, teacher interpretation and contextual constraints:

> Curriculum misalignment occurs when the elements of instructional design - learning outcomes, teaching strategies, and assessment methods - are not systematically aligned, leading to disjointed learning experiences that undermine the educational process.
>
> (Bull, 2025, p. 65)

An idea may seem great in principle, but how that idea is implemented and received by colleagues and other stakeholders is critical for how successful it will eventually be. It must be aspirational but also reflective on the school's community, values and ethos. Jones and Leagon (2014) emphasise that there are several factors that will affect how well an idea is received: 'teachers' prior knowledge and experience, self-efficacy, epistemic belief and the social cultural context of the teacher (Jones and Leagon, 2014).

Let's unpick this:

Teachers' prior knowledge and experience: What teachers already know and have lived through professionally - their subject knowledge; training, classroom experience and past successes or challenges. These influence how confidently and accurately they interpret and teach the curriculum.

Self-efficacy: This is a teacher's own self-confidence and their own ability to teach effectively. When this self-belief is high, teachers are more likely to try new approaches.

Epistemic belief: This takes into account teachers' own knowledge and beliefs. Is their knowledge fixed or open to change and evolving? What is their attitude to their own learning?

Social and cultural context of the teacher: What is the wider environment like for the teacher? This takes into consideration the school culture and leadership expectations. The curriculum accountability and assessment pressures. The school demographics and local community. These factors will affect what teachers feel about what they are teaching.

To help implement new ideas and review where your curriculum currently is, the Education Endowment Foundation suggests the following ways to help smooth the adoption of something new: engage, unite and reflect. The image below illustrates this plan.

What Does a 'Broad and Balanced' Curriculum Mean?

Broad and balanced are terms which are used to reading and hearing about when considering curriculum planning and the National Curriculum more widely. These terms were first referenced legally in 1988, in the Education Reform Act:

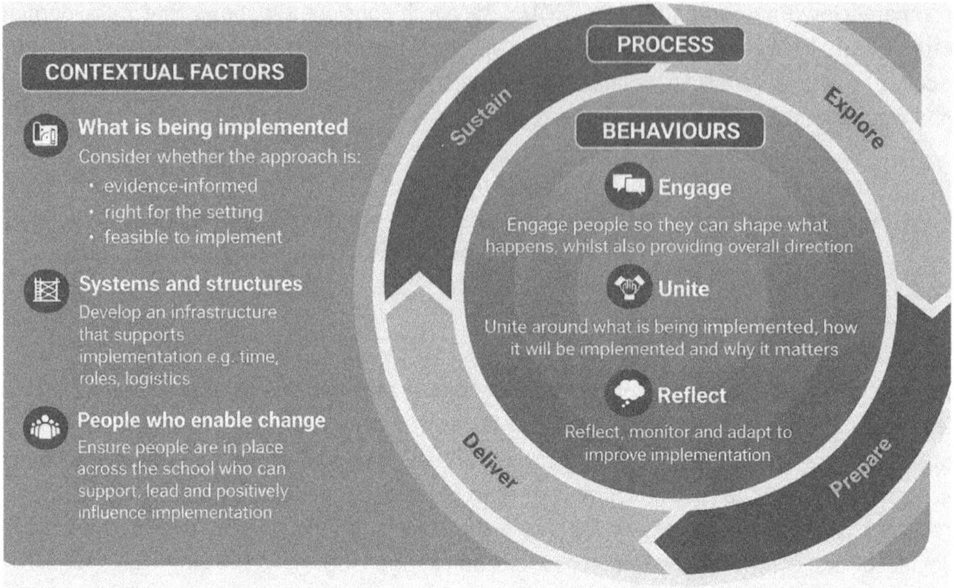

Figure 8.1 Putting evidence to work: A school's guide to implementation

(Education Endowment Foundation 2019)

> a balanced and broadly based curriculum which (a) promotes the spiritual, moral, cultural, mental and physical development of pupils at the school and of society; and (b) prepares such pupils for the opportunities, responsibilities and experiences of adult life.
>
> (Education Reform Act 1988)

When the 2014 National Curriculum was introduced, the terms were mentioned explicitly as a legal requirement for all schools: 'every state-funded school must offer a curriculum which is "balanced and broadly based"' (Department for Education, 2014). However, there does not seem to be an actual definition of these terms, and it could be argued these are fairly vague terms. So, what does a broad and balanced curriculum actually mean?

We could surmise that a *broad* curriculum offers students a wide range of subjects, experiences and enrichment opportunities in which they can develop, grow and learn, not just in the moment, but that help develop and prepare the young people for the future. In contrast to this, a narrowing of the curriculum might imply that the subjects are narrow and limiting. A *balanced* curriculum one might say gives equal consideration to all subjects. Certainly, deciding what to include when considering curriculum design is a value judgement. For example, do you plan across subjects instead of teaching geography and history separately or, teach under the term, humanities? What skills need to be emphasised and taught?

Think now about how a 'broad' curriculum is taught in your school or setting? When do you hear these terms?

Powerful Knowledge

While the notion of a broad and balanced curriculum emphasises the breadth and depth of what should be taught, these terms do not, on their own, address questions about the nature or purpose of the knowledge which is taught. A curriculum may appear broad in terms of coverage yet still need to address which knowledge is selected to be taught and whose knowledge is valued.

It is at this point that the concept of powerful knowledge becomes significant. Rather than focusing solely on breadth or balance, powerful knowledge draws attention to the kinds of disciplinary knowledge that allow learners to think beyond their everyday experiences, make sense of ideas and participate more fully in society. From this perspective, curriculum design is not only about ensuring coverage across subjects, but about making deliberate choices regarding the knowledge that has the greatest potential to empower learners for their future.

What Is Powerful Knowledge?

Michael Young (2009) defines powerful knowledge as having two key characteristics: It is *specialised* in how it is produced and it is *differentiated* from the experiences of the students. It is 'powerful' because it is near to being 'universal' (Young, 2011).

Young (2009) poses the question: 'What do students have an entitlement to learn?' He explains that the purpose of the curriculum is to transmit past knowledge to the next generation. Therefore, the key here is defining the important knowledge that pupils should be able to acquire in school and this is what is known as 'powerful knowledge'. Educators should, Young argues, be able to answer this question and design their own curriculum (within the framework of the National Curriculum). Contrary to this opinion, White (2012) believes that schools need to provide a reason why their central aim should be access to the concepts peculiar to academic subjects. White feels that the statement, to provide 'powerful knowledge', is not a justification 'but something closer to a tautology' (White, 2012). He elaborates this further and asks: Which academic subjects generate this powerful knowledge and how do we decide?

Case Study: How We Built a Curriculum That Opens Up the World for Our Children

Burnham-on-Crouch Primary School

Louise Boroughs - Deputy Head Teacher

At Burnham-on-Crouch Primary School, we often say that our curriculum is shaped by our children. Many of them arrive with limited life experiences and opportunities to travel beyond the local area and, for some, limited access to rich language and culture at home. We wanted a curriculum that didn't just fill these gaps – but opened doors, built confidence and gave every child the chance to see themselves in a bigger world.

Starting with What Our Children Need Most

When we designed our curriculum, we began by asking: What do our children need to thrive? Our curriculum intent makes this clear – pupils need to feel connected, inspired and able to access experiences that broaden their horizons.

We built our curriculum around a set of 'Golden Threads', including enrichment, multicultural understanding, creativity, critical thinking and future aspirations. These aren't extras – they're woven into everything we do. From Early Years to Year 6, we want children to feel excited, curious and able to see the world from different perspectives.

This approach was recognised in our 2025 Ofsted report, which praised the curriculum for being 'highly ambitious, well-designed and accessible to all'. Inspectors especially highlighted how much our children gain from the enrichment woven through our wider curriculum.

Our Two-Week Cycle: Giving Learning Time to Breathe

One of the unique ways we deliver our curriculum is through a two-week cycle for our foundation subjects. We noticed that children needed more time to really get stuck into learning – so this structure allows them to explore topics in greater depth rather than skimming through.

Each unit starts with a knowledge organiser that lays out the key vocabulary, big ideas and links to previous learning; children activate their prior learning through retrieval practice and discussion to help make connections between the topics that they study. Teachers refer back to the knowledge organiser throughout the fortnight so children can build and connect knowledge gradually. Lessons are sequenced so pupils can revisit ideas, make sense of them and genuinely remember what they've learned.

At the end of each cycle, children complete a short, low-stakes quiz. It isn't high-pressure – just a way for us to check what's stuck and what needs a little more time. It helps us make sure no child is left behind.

And the most important part? Every single two-week block includes an enrichment experience. We wanted to guarantee that enrichment wasn't something that happened 'if there was time', but part of the learning journey for every child.

Enrichment: The Beating Heart of Our Curriculum

Our enrichment offer is what families talk about most – and what children remember: 100% of our curriculum units include enrichment, and children and parents overwhelmingly say these experiences boost learning.

Across a single year, children experience an extraordinary breadth of opportunities:

STEM & Science *– robotics projects, CSI forensic science workshops, VR expeditions, engineering days, 'Living Eggs', and outdoor science.*
History & Geography *– fieldwork on local rivers, Stone Age and Roman workshops, trips to Colchester Castle, Duxford, and London museums.*
Arts & Culture *– Hindu dance, circus skills, whole-school art exhibitions, Young Voices at the O2, specialist music tuition and arts residencies.*
Community & Citizenship *– visits from emergency services, NSPCC workshops, first aid training, civic engagement projects, and wellbeing days.*
Sport & Outdoor Learning *– sports festivals, inflatables days, outdoor adventures such as 'Call of the Wild', and a Year 6 residential.*

These moments aren't add-ons – they're part of how we help children feel connected to the world.

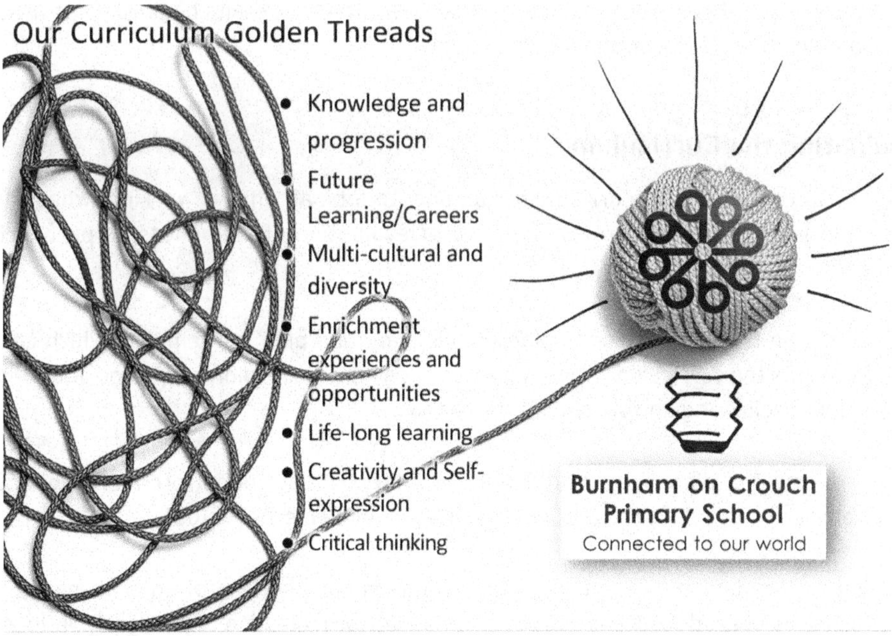

Figure 8.2 Our curriculum of golden threads

What This Means for Our Children

The impact is visible every day. Children talk confidently about their learning, recall knowledge deeply and show huge pride in their experiences. Foundation outcomes remain strong, and pupils' engagement with the curriculum is exceptionally high.

Most importantly, our curriculum now gives every child - not just the most advantaged - the chance to dream bigger, see more and feel that the world is open to them.

Case study question: To what extent does our curriculum deliberately respond to the lived experiences of our pupils, ensuring that enrichment and powerful learning opportunities are embedded as entitlement for all rather than optional additions?

The following templates are designed to support the analysis process. They provide structured opportunities to evaluate your current curriculum, assess the skills being taught in your school, identify disadvantaged groups within your context and begin shaping a vision for inclusive, future-focused provision.

Evaluating the Curriculum

In order to evaluate your curriculum planning; to look at what is working, what needs adapting, you might want to use a model of evaluative effectiveness as part of this process:

The Education Endowment Foundation's Implementation plan is a template which can be used to assess the curriculum. This plan focuses on an initial exploration stage, followed by preparation, delivering and sustaining the change.

You can view the plan here: https://d2tic4wvo1iusb.cloudfront.net/production/eef-guidance-reports/implementation/a_schools_guide_to_implementation.pdf

Leading and implementing organisational change is complex and often challenging. The way change is introduced and received within an organisation significantly influences whether it becomes embedded or fades over time. Models such as Kotter's Change Model (1996) provide a structured framework to support sustainable implementation. Dr John Kotter proposed an eight-step process designed to guide leaders in successfully planning, managing and securing long-term change.

Evaluation	*Questions*	*Evidence*
Student experience of the curriculum	How do students perceive the curriculum? • To what extent does it feel relevant, inclusive and engaging? • What do students identify as missing?	Student voice surveys Focus groups Attendance patterns
Impact on progress and attainment & student wellbeing	What measurable impact does the curriculum have on attainment and progress? • Which groups benefit most/least? • What structural or pedagogical factors limit stronger outcomes?	Assessment data Progress measures Disadvantage gaps
Contribution to Pastoral and Wellbeing Needs	How effectively does the curriculum support students' emotional, social and behavioural development? • Where are there gaps between curriculum intent and lived experience? • How well does curriculum design align with safeguarding and inclusion principles?	Behaviour data Safeguarding records Student wellbeing surveys Staff reflections

Figure 8.3 Curriculum Evaluation Framework

(Adapted from Kara, 2024, p. 33)

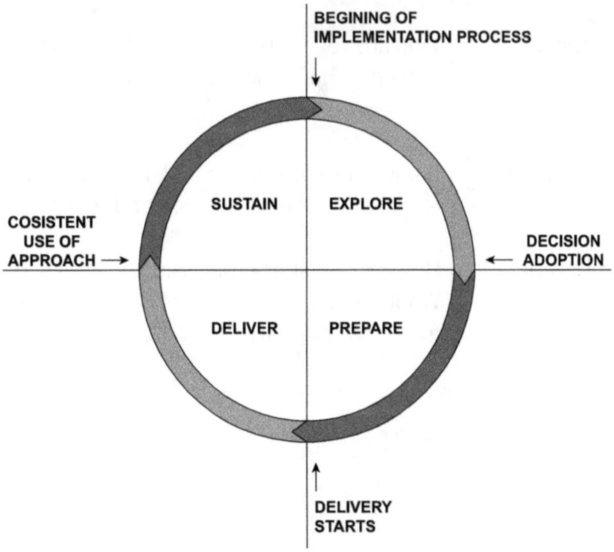

Figure 8.4 Implementation template

(Adapted from EEF, 2024)

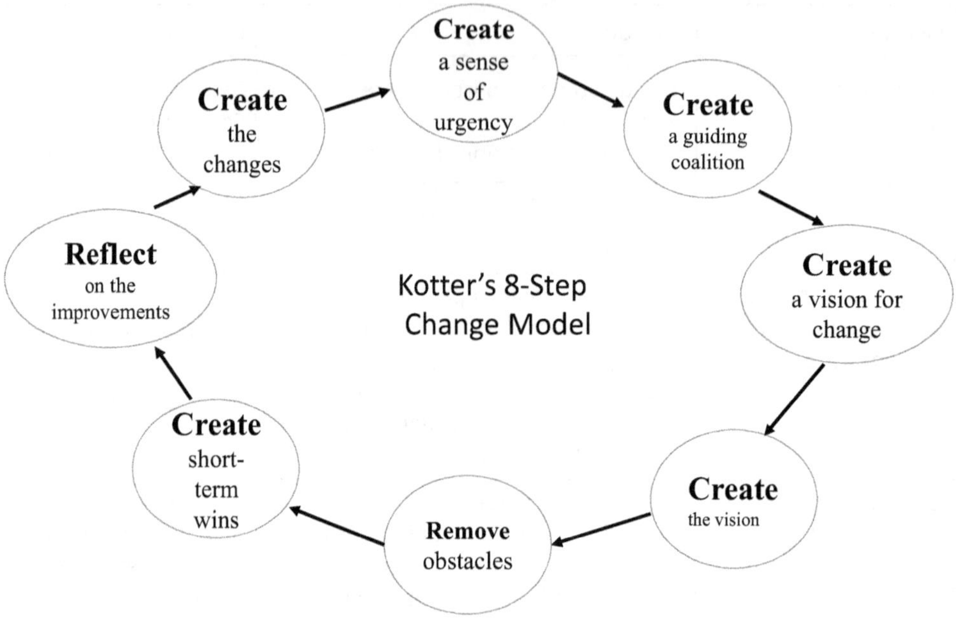

Figure 8.5 Kotter's Eight-Step Change Model

(Adapted from Kotter, 1996)

Change step	*Questions*
Create urgency	How can we let people know this work is important? What is the persuasive element here? How do we ensure people know it matters?
Form a powerful coalition	Who are your early adopters? Who has the expertise and will to help? Who has influence that could drive this forward?
Create a vision for change	What does the change look like? What is the big picture for all of us? What will look and feel different as a result?
Communicate the vision	How can we share this vision without it being a slogan? What do people need to hear and focus on? Where will it exist? Whose voices need to be heard?

Figure 8.6 Applying Kotter's Eight-Step Change Model to curriculum reform

(Adapted from Kara, 2024, p. 57; based on Kotter, 1996)

Empower action	How can we facilitate change? What space/time needs to be given to this change? How can we provide a sense of autonomy while sticking to our values?
Create quick wins	What will create momentum? What will keep people from flagging along the way? How will we celebrate the quick wins?
Build on the change	How do we add depth to the change? How will we commit to ongoing conversation? What will be our accountability and support measures?
Make it stick	How can we ensure the change is sustained? How can we make the change a cultural shift? How is it going to become the core of who we are?

Figure 8.6 (Continued)

Skills Audit of the Curriculum

Below is the skills audit of the curriculum referred to in Chapter 6. This audit invites you to examine key questions:

- What skills are we intentionally developing across our curriculum?
- Which pupils are accessing and strengthening these skills and who may be missing out?
- Are the skills we prioritise aligned with the realities of our community and the futures our pupils will enter?

Skills Audit of the Curriculum

Skill	*Evidence in Classroom Practice*	*Evidence Across the School*	*Current Strength*	*Priority for Development*
Listening	Active listening tasks? Paired group discussions? Opportunities to respond and question?	School assemblies, tutor time, restorative practice, peer mentoring	☐ 1 ☐ 2 ☐ 3 ☐ 4 ☐ 5	
Speaking	Class debates, presentations, oral feedback, structured dialogue, poetry recital	Influential speakers, school council, performances, public speaking competitions Lamda	☐ 1 ☐ 2 ☐ 3 ☐ 4 ☐ 5	
Problem solving	Inquiry-based tasks, project work, maths/science challenges	Enterprise activities, STEM clubs, problem-based learning projects	☐ 1 ☐ 2 ☐ 3 ☐ 4 ☐ 5	
Creativity	Opportunities for art, creative writing, designing and innovation	Enrichment (arts, music, drama), cross-curricular projects, innovation days	☐ 1 ☐ 2 ☐ 3 ☐ 4 ☐ 5	
Staying positive	Growth mindset strategies, feedback culture, resilience tasks	Wellbeing programme, pastoral support, rewards systems	☐ 1 ☐ 2 ☐ 3 ☐ 4 ☐ 5	
Aiming high	Stretch/ challenge tasks, goal-setting, mastery learning	Careers guidance, mentoring, progression pathways, influential speakers, work experience, focus in school, assemblies	☐ 1 ☐ 2 ☐ 3 ☐ 4 ☐ 5	
Leadership	Group roles in projects, peer teaching, classroom responsibilities	Student leadership roles, prefects, ambassadors	☐ 1 ☐ 2 ☐ 3 ☐ 4 ☐ 5	

Teamwork	Collaborative tasks, peer assessment, cooperative learning	Sports teams, music ensembles, house competitions, projects in lessons	☐ 1 ☐ 2 ☐ 3 ☐ 4 ☐ 5	

Diversity and Inclusion Audit

The Diversity and Inclusion audit is referred to in Chapter 5. The audit invites you to reflect on:

- Whose voices are consistently represented across subjects?
- Where are perspectives limited, stereotyped or absent?
- Does your curriculum reflect both local community context and global diversity?
- How are issues of race, gender, disability, socio-economic background and culture meaningfully embedded rather than added on?

Diversity and Inclusion Audit

1. Reevaluate your teaching materials. Are the texts being taught to your pupils relevant? What voices are being promoted within your classroom/subject/school/setting?	
2. What steps can we take to ensure that students feel connected to what they are learning about?	
3. What opportunities for real-life experiences are being planned for?	
4. How is your school unlocking skills that children will need for the future?	
5. How are you organising seating plans?	
6. Do you pre-teach? How could this be organised?	
7. Give students agency – what would they like to see?	
8. Reach out to other schools in your area who have started/already diversified and decolonised their curriculum.	
9. Ensure you are creating a safe space for discussion.	
10. How are interventions completed? Organised?	

Vocabulary Development

Strategies for Talk	*Description*
Sentence stems	Provide examples of speaking structures around the classroom. These provide a lead in for children: First, At the beginning, In my opinion, Following on from what . . . Said . . . I believe, in my opinion . . . I wonder if, I don't believe
Think Pair Share	This gives students the opportunity to explore their thinking before speaking in a big group.
A word or phrase a day	Place a word by the door. As the students enter or leave the classroom, they have to say the word out loud.
Talk roles	In pairs or a group assign specific roles to students. 1. Instigator - will start the discussion 2. Prober - asks for more detail 3. Challenger - puts forward another view point or a different opinion 4. Clarifyer - sums up the discussion

Bereavement and Loss

Loss is an inevitable part of life, yet it is often the least planned-for experience within school systems.

For many children, school is the most stable environment in their lives. When bereavement occurs, the way a school responds can either strengthen a child's sense of belonging and safety, or compound feelings of isolation and uncertainty. A clear, compassionate bereavement policy ensures that support is not improvised in moments of crisis but thoughtfully prepared in advance.

This example policy is designed to help schools move from reactive responses to intentional pastoral care.

An example bereavement policy from Winston's Wish - their website can be found here: winstonswish.org

TICK hub **Pupil Premium Progress Tracker**

Name:	**DOB:**	**Date joined school:**
EAL: Yes/ No	**SEN: Yes/ No**	**PP: Yes/No**
Met GLD: Yes/No	**Accessed any S&L intervention in EYFS: Yes/ No (if so which)**	
On track at end of KS1: Yes/No	**Passed Phonics test: Yes/No**	
On track at end of KS2: Yes/ No	**Passed Timetable test: Yes/No**	

Early Years Foundation Stage:
Initial needs assessment:

Chapter Takeaways

Reflections

- The conceptualisation of curriculum as *currere* - a race course or pathway - is a powerful metaphor that reframes curriculum as a lived journey rather than a static document. Viewing curriculum in this way foregrounds progression, sequencing and purpose, prompting reflection on whether learners are merely moving through content or genuinely developing understanding at each stage.
- The concept of curriculum misalignment is particularly significant, as it reveals how gaps between outcomes, pedagogy and assessment can undermine learning, even when curriculum design appears sound. This reinforces the idea that curriculum success does not lie solely in policy design, but in how teachers understand and enact it in context.
- Teachers' prior knowledge and experience influence not only what they teach, but how confidently and creatively they interpret curriculum expectations. Self-efficacy emerges as a critical factor: without belief in their own capacity, teachers may resist innovation or revert to safer, more familiar practices.
- Reflecting on this debate of what powerful knowledge to include reinforces the need for schools to articulate clear rationales for their curriculum choices, ensuring that breadth is matched by depth.
- Reflecting on curriculum implementation through a Kotter lens highlights the importance of teacher buy-in at the meso level of curriculum enactment. If teachers do not understand the rationale for change or feel excluded from decision-making, even well-designed curriculum reforms are unlikely to result in meaningful classroom practice.

Now Consider

- Which policies do you have in school, and do they need updating and sharing with the school's governors?
- What is the sequence of events that take place in the event of a bereavement? Is this covered if staff are absent and are all staff aware of their roles?
- How do you practise and help staff understand how to deal with a medical emergency?
- Consider having an emergency system in place if there is a medical emergency. Perhaps green cards for minor emergencies so a staff member can be informed and red cards for a critical emergency when any staff must come immediately. How is a system like this shared with children and staff?
- How is enrichment planned and delivered to support all children and adults in the school community?

Enhanced Provision and Ideas to Support Learning

- A coherently sequenced curriculum that supports progression and cumulative knowledge and skills.
- Deliberate identification and teaching of powerful knowledge and skills within each subject.
- Alignment between curriculum intent, implementation and assessment.
- Inclusive provision that meets the needs of all learners, including SEND and disadvantaged pupils.
- Ongoing review, professional development and reflection to sustain effective practice.

Bibliography

Bull, D.A. (2025). 'Impact of curriculum misalignment and assessment practices on student learning outcomes in higher education: A PRISMA-guided qualitative content synthesis'. *International Journal of Interdisciplinary Research and Innovations*, 13(3), 65–87. https://doi.org/10.5281/zenodo.16262451.

Department for Education. (2014). *The national curriculum in England: Framework document*. London: Department for Education. https://assets.publishing.service.gov.uk/media/5a7b3d8ded915d4147620d6b/PRIMARY_national_curriculum.pdf.

Education Endowment Foundation (EEF). (2024). *Implementation planning template*. London: Education Endowment Foundation.

Jones, G.M. and Leagon, M. (2014). 'Science teacher attitudes and beliefs: Reforming practice', in N.G. Lederman and S.K. Abell (eds.), *Handbook of research on science education*. New York and London: Routledge, pp. 830–847.

Kara, B. (2024). *The diverse curriculum*. London: SAGE Publications Ltd.

Kotter, J.P. (1996). *Leading change*. Boston, MA: Harvard Business School Press.

Phaeton, M.J. and Stears, M. (2017). 'Exploring the alignment of the intended and implemented curriculum through teachers' interpretation: A case study of A-Level Biology practical work'. *Eurasia Journal of Mathematics, Science and Technology Education*, 13(3), 723–740.

White, J. (2012). 'Powerful knowledge: Too weak a prop for the traditional curriculum?', *New Visions for Education Group Research and Development Series*. Institute of Education, University of London. https://www.newvisionsforeducation.org.uk/wp-content/uploads/2017/03/Powerful-Knowledge-too-weak-a-prop-for-the-traditional-curriculum-John-White.pdf.

Wikipedia – Curriculum. (2026). *Curriculum*. https://en.wikipedia.org/wiki/Curriculum.

Young, M. (2011). 'The return to subjects: A sociological perspective on the UK knowledge-based curriculum'. *Curriculum Journal*, 22(3), 265–278. https://doi.org/10.1080/09585176.2011.582687.

Final Thoughts

What is taught in schools has been debated since the dawn of education. The National Curriculum and the Early Years Foundation Stage Framework reflect what we, as a country, value, who we prioritise and what we envisage a future will look like - where all children can be successful, lifelong learners

At a time when change is on the horizon for education, new policies are being published, as well as a new National Curriculum. It is imperative that we continue to design a curriculum which is inspiring for today's children. If we continue to design a curriculum which safely maintains the status quo, the children who need the opportunities the most will continue to experience education as something done to them, rather than helping and equipping them.

This is a call for courageous curriculum leadership and ask the questions:

- Who is this curriculum and curricula truly serving?Whose stories are visible?
- Whose potential is being limited by low expectations or unconscious bias?
- What opportunities, knowledge and skills will genuinely expand life chances?

Schools must be the bridge between where students are now and their future selves, there is no place in education for short-termism. We know that when children feel a deep sense of belonging and when schools plan enriching opportunities that pupils may not otherwise access then this can broaden horizons and raise barriers. Raising barriers to learning in all areas is not about lowering standards or expectations. It is about removing the obstacles that prevent children from reaching higher through equity not equality.

The school day is busy, there can be limited time, limited person power and class sizes are large. We can feel overrun with the immediate tasks which we need to complete. This task, providing a curriculum and education that is empowering and inclusive for all children, is not small. It requires self-reflection, honesty and perhaps bravery. When a curriculum is rooted in equity and community (among other things), then schools become places where all young people (and adults) are prepared to flourish in life.

DOI: 10.4324/9781003624004-9

INDEX

Bold page numbers indicate tables, *italic* numbers indicate figures.

For Product Safety Concerns and Information please contact our EU
representative GPSR@taylorandfrancis.com
Taylor & Francis Verlag GmbH, Kaufingerstraße 24, 80331 München, Germany

www.ingramcontent.com/pod-product-compliance
Lightning Source LLC
LaVergne TN
LVHW081311190926
848399LV00036B/369

* 9 7 8 1 0 4 1 0 3 4 7 3 5 *